Tell Them
We Are Rising

Tell Them We Are Rising

A Memoir of Faith in Education

Ruth Wright Hayre

and

Alexis Moore

Foreword by Ed Bradley

John Wiley & Sons, Inc.

New York • Chichester • Weinheim • Brisbane • Singapore • Toronto

Copyright © 1997 by Ruth Wright Hayre and Alexis Moore
Published by John Wiley & Sons, Inc.

Library of Congress Cataloging-in-Publication Data
Hayre, Ruth Wright
    Tell them we are rising : a memoir of faith in education / Ruth
  Wright Hayre and Alexis Moore.
        p.   cm.
    Includes index.
    ISBN 0-471-12679-9 (cloth : alk. paper)
    1. Hayre, Ruth Wright, 1910–   2. Afro-American women teachers—
  United States—Biography. 3. Public schools—Pennsylvania—
  Philadelphia. I. Moore, Alexis, 1951– . II. Title.
  LA2317.H49A3   1997
  371.1'0092—dc21
  [B]   97-1492

Printed in the United States of America

10 9 8 7 6 5 4 3 2 1

Dedicated to my parents
Richard Robert Wright Jr., 1878–1967
Charlotte Crogman Wright, 1879–1959

HOWARD AT ATLANTA

Right in the track where Sherman
  Ploughed his red furrow,
Out of the narrow cabin,
  Up from the cellar's burrow,
Gathered the little black people,
  With freedom newly dowered,
Where, beside their Northern teacher,
  Stood the soldier, Howard.

He listened and heard the children
  Of the poor and long-enslaved
Reading the words of Jesus,
  Singing the songs of David.
Behold!—the dumb lips speaking,
  The blind eyes seeing!
Bones of the Prophet's vision
  Warmed into being!

Transformed he saw them passing
  Their new life's portal!
Almost it seemed the mortal
  Put on the immortal.
No more with the beasts of burden,
  No more with stone and clod,
But crowned with glory and honor
  In the image of God!

There was the human chattel
  Its manhood taking;
There, in each dark, bronze statue,
  A soul was waking!
The man of many battles,
  With tears his eyelids pressing,
Stretched over those dusky foreheads
  His one-armed blessing.

And he said: "Who hears can never
  Fear for or doubt you;
What shall I tell the children
  Up North about you?"
Then ran round a whisper, a murmur,
  Some answer devising;
And a little boy stood up: "General,
  Tell 'em we're rising!"

O black boy of Atlanta!
  But half was spoken:
The slave's chain and the master's
  Alike are broken.
The one curse of the races
  Held both in tether:
They are rising—all are rising,
  The black and white together.

O brave men and fair women!
  Ill comes of hate and scorning:
Shall the dark faces only
  Be turned to morning—
Make Time your sole avenger,
  All-healing, all-redressing;
Meet Fate half-way, and make it
  A joy and blessing!

           John Greenleaf Whittier

Contents

Foreword

I HAVE A SPECIAL FONDNESS for Dr. Ruth Hayre. She paved the way for my career in journalism. When I was a young sixth-grade teacher with only three years experience in the Philadelphia school system, she approved my appointment as acting vice-principal at the Mann School. It was a temporary assignment that would last only until the end of that school year. The following September, I would have to go back into the classroom. At the time I was working at a small radio station in Philadelphia and trying to decide what I wanted to do with my life: education or broadcasting. Her faith in me and exposure to life out of the classroom made my decision easy.

Ruth Hayre comes from a long line of educators and a tradition of education. In her own school years, she always occupied seat one row one, which went to the student with the highest average. She knew early on that she wanted to be a teacher. After fifty years as a teacher, principal, and school board president she thought she knew the score. She admits she didn't. The six years with her Risers drove home the difference between her days as a young person and life for kids today. This book focuses on her life and education and a career that has spanned the remarkable as well as the terrible changes in our inner cities and the children who live there.

Giving back became an obsession for her. *Tell Them We Are Rising* is the inspiring story of how one woman gave back. As she says, "It is a worthy coda to a lifelong educational adventure."

Ed Bradley

Acknowledgments

T HERE ARE PEOPLE WHO HAVE HELPED ME in many ways in the writing of this book. Alexis Moore Bruton, my coauthor, has added so much to its ultimate development. In fact, it would never have come to pass if I had not said in a casual encounter, "How about you and me writing a book?" I was surprised at her almost immediate enthusiasm for the project. It was my "voice" that she insisted be maintained. But it was her writing and rewriting that produced the hundreds of pages of material sent to the editors. Many of the stories and much of the material about our "Risers" (those 116 school pupils who entered my life) were the result of her interviews with the children, as well as others in the book. And her husband, Mike Bruton, was a help in many ways.

I acknowledge, with thanks, the support of Hana Umlauf Lane, Senior Editor of John Wiley and Sons, Inc., who read our first proposal and recognized the possibilities in the book. For almost three years, Hana has worked carefully and devotedly with Alexis and me.

We also acknowledge two other important members of the Wiley team, Carole Hall and Audreen Buffalo Ballard, who worked closely with the manuscript.

I acknowledge those 116 students who came out of the sixth grade in 1988. Without their emergence into my life, I am sure there would have been no story, or no book. Each one of them deserves a story of his or her own.

I acknowledge the mentors, that group of over 130 men and women who served our children in so many ways. Among those whose contributions are described in the book are Joan Harris, Shirley Tyree, Arthur J. Wells, Elvedine Wilkerson, Gladys Blackwell, Jean Chandler, Ethel Clark, Ronnie Collins, Stuart Cooperstein, Dr. Alma Crocker, Dr. Ida Dark, April Easley, Dr. Leonard Finkelstein, Gwen Florio, Frederick Foard, Kenneth A. Harper, Sylvia Harrison, Ronald James, Lucille Kornegay, Dannie Lipscomb, Ernest Lowe, Rev. Rose Martin, Dr. Edna McCrae, Earl Morgan, Edith Nimmons, Lucille Oliver, Charles Patterson, Hilderbrand Pelzer, Claudia Pharis, Terrel Parris, Dr. Raymond Ragland, Dr. Mary W. Reid, Annette Sample, Bessie Session, Lawrence Small-wood, Edith Moore Stephens, Doris Thornton, Elizabeth Trulear, and Margaret McLaughlin.

We appreciate the dedicated efforts of Mrs. Deloris James, the coordinator of the program, as well as Dr. Richard Englert, the first dean of Temple University College of Education, in 1988–1989, and his successor, Dr. Trevor Sewell, who guided the project from 1989 until the present day. Also long-term affiliates of the College were Dr. John Shapiro and Dr. Joseph DuCett.

We thank for their interest and assistance former Congressman Bill Gray, Charles Greene of the Bell Telephone Company, and Ed Bradley of *60 Minutes.*

Many teachers, principals, and counselors have also been involved, especially counselors Charlotte Robinson at Dobbins and Anne Myers at Gratz High School; also principals Deidre Farmbry and Karen DelGuercio.

My thanks to Dr. Jeanette Brewer and Mrs. Madeline Cartwright, to Sylvia Hayre Harrison and J. Elizabeth Morgan, and to Dr. Constance Clayton and Dr. Peter Liacouras for their encouragement over the years.

Ruth W. Hayre

Tell Them We Are Rising

Chapter 1

"Tell Them We
Are Rising"

HERE I AM AT AGE 83, writing the first sentence of a book. It isn't easy, but it's a challenge, and I've always been a sucker for a challenge. My dad, himself a writer and editor, used to suggest that I become a writer. Instead, I chose to teach, a secure, income-producing profession, one of the few such open to black women of my generation. Write a book? When? I was much too busy living my life to sit and write about it. Besides, I didn't feel I had anything exceptional to tell.

My feelings would begin to change in 1988 following graduation ceremonies at two Philadelphia elementary schools. I had chosen a splendid June day to make an announcement I had mulled over secretly for more than a year. Anxiously I took my seat on stage at Wright Elementary School. Parents, friends, teachers, and tots filled the

1

Making my big announce-
ment at the graduation
ceremony at Richard
Robert Wright School,
1988.

auditorium that doubled as the school cafeteria. Anticipation was keen as we awaited the proud march of the sixth-grade class of 1988. Slowly and shyly, the graduating students entered, girls from the left, boys from the right. They marched two by two down the aisle to applause and cheers so spirited that the strains of "Pomp and Circumstance" coming from a loudspeaker were almost drowned out.

After being introduced, I congratulated the graduates, affirmed my faith in their abilities, and made the vow I had set so long ago as my goal. That day I promised 116 sixth-grade graduates from two schools in the city's toughest neighborhoods that when they completed high school, I would pay their college tuition.

Before I completed my pledge that began, "Funds will be used almost exclusively to pay the tuition for each student in the June 1988 graduating class . . ." an electrical charge seemed to galvanize the crowd. By the time I concluded with ". . . who is accepted into an accredited college or other post–high school program," the audience was on its feet. Teachers cheered, parents wept, journalists shouted questions. Television lights glared and the children stood dazed. Happy pandemonium reigned. A few hours later I made the same vow to graduating students at Kenderton Elementary School and met with the same elated reception. That day nothing seemed impossible.

This is the story of our journey—116 boys and girls and one octogenarian teacher-administrator-grandmother—through the next six years of public school life. It is also a story about my "leap of faith" and the family and traditions that inspired a gift I hoped would change the lives of these children I call the Risers.

I did not embark on this mission as a starry-eyed do-gooder. I was no stranger to the problems of single-parent homes or the realities of contemporary adolescent life. I had more than fifty years under my belt as teacher, principal, and school board president, and I thought I knew the score. But at the time, I would have scoffed at any prediction that I could become utterly absorbed in the lives of children whose worlds were wildly different from mine.

I would learn over the next six years that there were many differences between inner-city adolescents circa 1990 and my own sheltered and supervised coming of age seventy years earlier. Many of my Risers had learned bitter adult lessons at a very early age. Their fatalistic acceptance of the possibility of death at an early age was but one of our many dissimilarities. Their competence at tasks I never had to tackle—like making a slim government check feed a family for two weeks—still strike me as inspiring.

This is a book about winning. It is also a book about loss—but not about losing. The stories in these pages are as varied as the dilemmas, temptations, and opportunities that confront urban students today. You will meet one young boy so determined to attend the high school of his choice that he trekked six hours to and from classes each day. Such single-minded determination rarely goes unrewarded. He won acceptance to the college of his dreams. Another, faced with his mother's sudden death, went into a tailspin, then rallied to pull himself into a bright future. A young girl raised her brothers and sisters in a home where chaos was a constant, yet she managed to graduate on time. Another girl—a brilliant child—decided to dance in a nude bar rather than pursue the offered scholarship. Their stories reflect incredible strengths, sorrows, the gift of mother wit, and the resilience of grace. They are all indelibly fixed in my mind and my heart.

This book is about Teneshia, Wendell, Shawn, Yvonne, Jeannette, Latika, Hasaan, and the many other students who managed to overcome severe disadvantages and catch hold of the dream that my pledge promised. Today they are in college—my dream for them—and I am writing— my father's dream for me—about our journey together.

People often ask how I was able to fund the Risers. My husband and I, both teachers, were prudent savers throughout our marriage. We invested our resources, which were supplemented from time to time with a modest bequest from my father. When my husband passed away, he left a respectable estate on which I could live quite comfortably. These assets, further invested to capitalize on the economic incentives initiated during the Reagan years, left me with more money than I could use in my lifetime. This permitted me to underwrite the Risers program.

My bequest and challenge to the Risers is built foursquare on the cornerstones of racial and familial traditions.

"Liberation through education" has been a tenet of black thought—in circumstances both straitened and flush—ever since our ancestors were enslaved and carried off to lands foreign in custom and culture. This belief that true liberation would only come through education was codified in the Emancipation Proclamation. Blacks, eager to revoke the stranglehold of slavery, zealously pursued the document's premise of education, often in the face of violent opposition. Schools known as freedom schools, or colored schools, were established in converted railroad boxcars from the Deep South to the Mason-Dixon line. Hundreds of people, hungry for the keys to freedom that education unlocked, tore themselves away from their families and walked miles, half-starved, to the closest boxcar school, where dedicated white missionary women taught the rudiments of knowledge—the alphabet, parsing sentences, and counting sums.

My paternal grandfather, Richard Robert Wright, became one of these students. His newly emancipated mother, Harriet, had marched him more than two hundred miles to Atlanta, where the school she knew he needed, and the learning she was determined he should have, was housed in a discarded railroad car. The journey took six months. Harriet, a good cook and all-around domestic servant, could pick up work and shelter by the day as they walked steadily toward Atlanta.

Richard, a shy, scrawny child made more so by the rigors of their march, shared a desk, a slate, and whatever precious book was available—usually a Bible—with many other pupils in that stifling metal school. Barefoot, clothed in remnants and patches, students shared food, tattered garments—whatever they had. Despite deplorable physical conditions—one water bucket for each school, no paper, no ventilation—Richard and his comrades plowed on,

The log cabin near Dalton, Georgia, in which my grandfather Richard Robert Wright was born.

determined to unlock the power of the word. Literacy was their goal, and often their god.

Funding for these schools was ordinarily provided by Northern white benefactors. General Oliver Otis Howard, a Union Army officer, was a patron of Richard Robert Wright's boxcar schoolroom. Howard would go on to head the Freedmen's Bureau and, later, to become the first president of the school that bears his name, Howard University.

Despite the chaos that reigned during the post–Civil War period, the general took a lively interest in the boxcar pupils and made regular rounds of the schools. During these trips Howard solicited progress reports that he used

General Oliver Otis Howard, the Union army officer and patron of Richard Robert Wright's boxcar school. He went on to head the Freedmen's Bureau and later to become the first president of the school that bears his name, Howard University. (Library of Congress)

to woo funds from other benefactors. On one such tour, Howard came to my grandfather's school.

General Howard's military bearing, flowing beard, and spit-and-polish appearance intimidated just about everyone. Imagine the fluttering schoolteachers and the overawed pupils as Howard strode to the front of the box-car and in the booming voice of field command asked, "Now, what message shall I take back North?"

Seamless silence, embarrassing to both teachers and students, hung in the air.

Finally, skinny, ragged Richard Robert Wright rose from his seat in the back of the room and raised his hand. After receiving an acknowledging nod from Howard, he made the remark that would eventually echo across the land.

"Sir, tell them we are rising."

The general did indeed take the message North. The poet John Greenleaf Whittier, on hearing the story, immortalized it in the poem "General O. O. Howard at Atlanta."

I have done my part by telling the tale as often and to as many people as possible. In June 1988, in a leap of faith not unlike my grandfather's, I named the program "Tell Them We Are Rising." It was humbling to be able to make my announcement at the school named in honor of my grandfather, the Richard Robert Wright Elementary School.

Once my ancestors acquired that precious education, they never looked back. I thought this reverence for schooling was widespread among my people. After all, I reasoned, these kids have so much more going for them than that little ex-slave who went on to become a founder and president of Georgia State College and of a black-owned

Philadelphia bank. Surely the Risers' parents had passed on the reverence for education that gives purpose, shapes lives, defeats obstacles. And so it seemed until I encountered the heartbreaking problem children of the late 1980s.

This book is the story of my life in education. By extension, and in a larger sense, it documents the black school experience over the past eighty years. Much of that experience has been good. Much has been bad.

My lifelong educational odyssey, culminating with the Risers, was inevitable. It was born in the tradition and shaped by the values that previous generations of black Americans, regardless of class or circumstance, placed on learning. Educational achievement, coupled with the motif of helping one another, was the true criterion of class among blacks in preintegration America. These values are rooted in my family history and steeped in an inherited love of teaching and scholarship.

You have met my grandfather Wright, born a slave in approximately 1853 in the southern part of Georgia. Grandpa took to learning with a vengeance. Thirteen years after his boxcar education began, he completed his studies at Atlanta University, graduating with its first class. He never looked back.

His life is recorded in a 1952 biography, *Black Boy of Atlanta,* with considerable detail about his childhood during slavery. He often boasted that ancestors in his mother's line were chiefs of the Mandingo tribe. I've never had an opportunity to research this, but it was a compelling story as Grandpa told it. I do know that his father, Richard Waddell, was a strong and very independent coachman for a plantation owner. One day the master beat

My grandfather Richard Wright's family in 1901 when he was president of Georgia State College. My father is the oldest boy, in the middle in the top row.

him viciously and my great-grandfather fought back. To avoid an almost certain death penalty, he fled. Nothing more was heard of him. Harriet, a few years later, remarried Alexander Wright, and they bore two children. Richard was named Wright for his stepfather. According to the story, Alexander left Harriet and his family to join the Yankee army.

Grandpa Wright went on to become a founder of Georgia State College, formally named Georgia State Agricultural and Industrial College, and to serve as its president for more than thirty years. He retired at age 65. Then, encouraged by his son, my father Richard Jr., he moved to Philadelphia in 1921 and founded Citizens and

Grandpa Wright greeting four grandchildren with a government bond each at the bank he founded.

Southern Bank, remaining its president until his death in 1947 at age 94.

My maternal grandfather, William H. Crogman, had a very different history. Since he rarely spoke of his childhood, I know little about his early life except that he was born in St. Maarten in the West Indies on May 1, 1841, and was an orphan, born free. When he was 14 he joined a ship's crew and sailed the seven seas. I found the only hint of his ancestry in "Talks for the Times," a collection of his speeches published in 1896. In an address celebrating the twenty-sixth anniversary of the Emancipation Proclamation, he recalled:

My grandfather on my mother's side, I know, was an Englishman whose name was Chippendale. Some years ago, when I was in the city of Liverpool, England, I saw this name on several signboards over the doors of business establishments, and was almost tempted to call in and claim kinship; but feared lest the effect of semitropical suns on my countenance might have rendered difficult the recognition of even a blood relative. I never knew my paternal grandfather, but a few years ago a German assured me that his grandfather imported the surname which I bear [Crogman] to this country from Bremen.

His life at sea ended after ten years, when he disembarked in Boston. His employer, impressed with his alert intelligence, offered to pay his school expenses, and Grandfather Crogman began his formal education in "the home of the bean and the cod." Eventually he traveled to Atlanta, where he, too, enrolled in Atlanta University's first class. He and Grandpa Wright were classmates and became lifelong friends.

For a while their paths separated. Grandfather Crogman went on to teach Latin and Greek at Atlanta's Clark University. Grandpa Wright was named principal of Edmund Asa Ware High in Augusta, the first high school set up for the free black people of Georgia. They named the school after the president of Atlanta University, my grandfather's benefactor.

Both men married shortly after their careers were established. Each of my grandmothers had gone to the equivalent of a "normal school," a two-year college program. Grandpa Wright met his future wife, Lydia Elizabeth Howard, at Atlanta University. A native of Columbus, Georgia, she was enrolled in the Normal Department, probably for teacher training. In Grandpa's biography she is described as "a bright student who captured Richard

Grandfather Crogman, about 1910 in Atlanta, Georgia.

completely with her charming manner and lovely, refined voice."

It seemed that Lydia's father might not accept Richard Wright, the ex-slave, as a suitable son-in-law. Howard had a longer tenure as a free man, having worked hard to purchase his freedom before slavery's end. He was the owner and operator of a carriage company and would make it known—often during the most ordinary conversation—that he had been a free Negro during slavery. With Lydia's help, Richard managed to win the old man over, and when Grandpa Wright graduated from Atlanta University, the two married. Although my grandmother's lovely oval face and velvet brown complexion won many compliments, what I remember best about her were her stately poise and unflappable temperament. She and my grandfather had eight children.

Like my grandmother Wright, my grandmother Crogman was also enrolled in the Normal Department of Atlanta University. A biography of Grandfather Crogman says about her that "in her character and service as his helpmeet, and as queen of one of the most refined and cultured homes, and the mother of eight most promising children, [she] is worthy of no less honor than the Professor himself." I know nothing of her parentage but I remember her as a handsome, statuesque woman with salt-and-pepper hair piled high in a braided crown.

For most of their lives the destinies of my two grandfathers were intertwined. They had similar traits: keen intellect, strong moral character, an insatiable thirst for learning, a commitment to improve the lives of black people, and a love and responsibility for family. They also shared many interests. Grandpa Wright organized the first Georgia State Fair in 1891. Four years later Grandfather

The Crogman family. This photo was taken about 1928 in my aunt's home in Kansas City, Missouri. My mother is on the right in the top row.

Crogman served as chairman of the first, and quite re-splendent, International State Exposition in Atlanta.

Yet they were different in several ways. Grandpa Wright was about 5′ 6″ and thin. As a child he had suffered from rickets and his health was fragile. He was dark and proud of it, often boasting of his pure African descent. Grandfather Crogman, fourteen years older, was taller, with a rich brown complexion, strong aquiline features, and an enviable crown of dark, wavy hair.

Their most observable differences lay in their temperaments. Grandpa Wright loved the limelight and courted its glare. He was born to lead, could "make a way out of no way," as they say, and had an unquenchable thirst for adventure. His biography gives a detailed account of his acquisition in 1939 of a four-passenger Wako airplane and its subsequent "Good Will Flight" with Charles Anderson, an extraordinary black pilot, at the controls.

Grandpa Wright, with his frail body and enormous mind and spirit, seemed to live a charmed life—frequently exposed to risk but always surviving. I sometimes wonder how he steered such an adroit course between the Scylla of entrenched intolerance and the Charybdis of racial violence that has proved so damaging to many other activist and outspoken blacks.

Grandfather Crogman, equally gifted, was quiet, contemplative, and unobtrusive. This careful, precise scholar of Latin and Greek was totally content to live his life at Clark University, where he eventually became president. My mother caught her father's enthusiasm for the classics and she, too, taught Latin and Greek at Clark until her marriage.

Grandfather Crogman was an active member of the Methodist Episcopal Church and served in several national positions. An 1896 volume of his speeches has given me insight into his philosophical wisdom. His inscription to me, *"Palme non sine pulvere,"* in a meticulous, flowing script, is translated at the top of the page, "They live forever who live for others."

My mother let us know that Grandfather Crogman was not only a scholar but a hero. A story she often told us about him was that when Atlanta issued the order that buses be segregated, he swore he would never ride city transportation again. It was a four-mile walk each way from the college to town. Although he was in his late sixties by then, he walked that walk. During the Atlanta riots early in this century, he bought a rifle and was prepared to use it on anyone who came to his house with harmful intentions. "He was always a courageous man," she told us.

I've told you these stories of my forebears—my great-grandmother Harriet, the slave mother who started the family's educational ball rolling, and my maternal and paternal grandparents, the Wrights and the Crogmans, because these are the people who gave me the breath of life. Their blood flows through my veins. They have given me their genes of intelligence and of longevity and the propensity to do the right thing. I am who I am because of them. Had they not existed, there would be no Risers program. Their inspiration, their tutelage, the example set by their indomitable spirit continue to guide me. These are the people who led me to a life in education.

Chapter 2

Root and Branch: The Family Tree

THERE WAS NEVER ANY QUESTION that I would become a teacher. I knew it the day I walked into my first-grade classroom in 1916. Although my teacher's face is lost to memory, I still recall the aura of disciplined calmness that ruled her classroom. Clearly this would be quite different from kindergarten. Each school day, I grew increasingly excited as she decoded the lines and circles of the alphabet to reveal words, which evolved into sentences, and then— glory of glories—books. I was convinced she was endowed with mystical talents, her mind the repository of magical secrets. These unfolding worlds gave me such exquisite pleasure that I could hardly wait for the next day's journey. If energy, discipline, and sheer desire were the profession's criteria, I knew what my work would be.

Teaching would be my calling, and as years passed, teaching would become my passion.

My ambition was entirely appropriate in the African American circle into which I was born. I was a child of some privilege, although I would not understand its responsibilities, burdens, and blessings until adolescence. My parents and paternal and maternal grandparents had earned undergraduate and graduate degrees. As you will see, any notion that I would not continue in the tradition was unthinkable.

My father, Richard Robert Wright Jr., was born on April 16, 1878. My mother, Charlotte Crogman, nicknamed Lottie and later "Miss Lottie," was born the following year on September 19.

When Lottie was 18, Richard Robert Wright Jr. came to Atlanta and met and fell in love with her. At the time my father was still finishing at Georgia State, but would later become a student at the Chicago Theological Seminary. It would be ten years before he had the means he thought necessary to care for a family. The promise of financial stability came when he accepted a position as the editor of the *Christian Recorder,* the official organ of the African Methodist Episcopal Church in Philadelphia. My parents married at the Crogman home on the campus of Clark University in 1909 and came to Philadelphia to live.

Life began for me on October 26, 1910, near the beginning of this eventful century now ending. Lynching was epidemic in the South. Segregation, de facto and de jure, was common. Even in enlightened Philadelphia definite racial parameters and distinctions, cultural and political, were observed in many aspects of our lives.

I think I look very intelligent in this picture taken in 1911. I am six months old.

Mama poses in her ostrich fur boa in 1940.

My mother had insisted I be born in her parents' home in Atlanta. When I was six weeks old, she returned to Philadelphia with me to discover that my father had bought a two-story house on a tree-lined street of immaculate houses in a predominantly white section of West Philadelphia. At the time, blacks accounted for less than 10 percent of the population. The majority lived, like most of my parents' friends, in North and South Philadelphia.

I remember little about that first house, but aspects of my family's early years are recorded in snapshots which, some eighty-three years later, I still find a delight. Some of them show a family Christmas celebration with a wonderfully decorated tree and, at its trunk, two or three dolls, one of them definitely black—surely one of the few in existence then. Other shots show me with my infant brother, Richard Robert Wright III, nicknamed Bunny, who was two years younger almost to the day.

Shortly afterwards, my father purchased a larger home across the street from the University of Pennsylvania complex, where he was studying for a doctorate in sociology. Our new home fascinated me. I particularly loved the fourth floor, where Dad stored items from his various entrepreneurial efforts, including samples from a black cosmetic company named Overton.

Mama found our new home a challenge. The four marble steps at the entrance, an architectural staple in many Philadelphia houses, had to be scrubbed daily. This was one of my chores until she insisted on covering them with a green wooden cover. Mama was a bit fragile and made it clear that she would need help. Susie Daniels, an old friend whose family owned a huge farm in Westminster, South Carolina, regularly recruited reliable young women who came North to help with the children and the housework. Mama still did all the cooking. Even today I remember her succotash, grits, fried fish, and chocolate layer cake, none of which I've ever managed to cook as well as she did.

The choice of a larger home had been carefully considered. My parents had relatives who wanted to attend Northern colleges, and our new home was roomy enough to receive them. My father's brother Whittier lived with us while attending medical school. So did Uncle Leon during his years as a dental school student at the University of Pennsylvania. His easy, laid-back personality satisfied all my requirements for the perfect uncle. My extraordinarily handsome Uncle Marcellus was enrolled at Temple when he died suddenly. He had inherited the strain of hemophilia that ran in my mother's family, eventually claiming four of her five brothers.

A room in our home was set aside for our out-of-town visitors, a custom of hospitality and a way around the indignities of discrimination. In those days blacks were routinely denied accommodation in white hotels. A. Philip Randolph, the great labor leader and civil rights activist, and Madam Evanti (Lillian Evans Tibbs), the glamorous operatic soprano, were among our many house guests. Madam C. J. Walker, the hair-care innovator and first black woman millionaire, made a lasting impression with her imposing demeanor and exquisite clothes. As she made her departure, my brother and sisters and I lined up to say goodbye, and she gave each of us a fifty-cent piece, a magnanimous gesture in those days.

Our house guests mirrored my father's several worlds, religious, political, cultural, and financial. His interests and involvements were reflections of Philadelphia's small but very strong middle class. The city could count a more than respectable number of black professionals—physicians, morticians, lawyers, teachers, and businesspeople. In 1908, my father compiled a directory of the city's black business owners. He counted more than eleven hundred, impressive for the time and perhaps even today.

Many black middle-class Philadelphians of that time were descendants of the small number of slaves who arrived with Dutch and English settlers in the late eighteenth and early nineteenth centuries. Legislation enacted in 1789 mandating the gradual abolition of slavery bore its first fruits early in the nineteenth century. Blacks who had been restricted previously to domestic and manual service branched out, becoming mechanics, seamen, carpenters, and skilled industrial workers. By 1820, they were home-owners and businesspeople who had developed a reputation for actively supporting black causes. They had initiated and sponsored their own institutions, both secular and ecclesiastical.

The African Methodist Episcopal Church, founded in Philadelphia in 1816 by Richard Allen, reflects that history. Born a slave in Philadelphia in 1765, Allen bought his freedom for two thousand dollars. A short time later he joined the ministry as an itinerant preacher. Initially a congregant of Olde St. George's, a white Methodist church in Philadelphia, he mounted a protest over the humiliating treatment of black worshipers, who were forced to sit in the church balcony. Allen led them from the church and subsequently established a place of worship in his black-smith shop. The church they built nearby exists today as Mother Bethel A.M.E Church. In 1816, the church became a national organization with Allen as its first elected bishop. Allen and his wife, Sarah, are buried at this historic site.

An ordained minister of the A.M.E Church and the editor of its official publication, my father was earnest and scholarly. Although "colored society" courted my parents, they had little interest in the dancing crowd. My father was made a member of what was supposed to be a select group of Philadelphia professionals known as the Boule. However, when he discovered that a light-skinned wife—my mother was fair—was one prerequisite for membership, he withdrew.

My mother and father were perfectly matched. Both were intelligent, loving, and reasonable. Mama had taught

My parents, Bishop R. R. Wright Jr. and Charlotte Crogman Wright, about 1945.

at Clark for almost ten years, but she was content to be a full-time wife and mother. For the first six years of their marriage, she was happily pregnant with me, my brother, Bunny, and my sisters Alberta Lavinia and Grace Lydia.

My parents insisted that everyone be present at each meal, even my father as busy as he was. Sunday afternoons we'd gather in the parlor, that solemn, special-occasion room, and listen to my father's classical records. His favorite artists were Roland Hayes, Marian Anderson, and Enrico Caruso. Caruso's rendition of "O Sole Mio," a staple of our Sunday afternoons, remains one of my musical favorites to this day.

We grew up on Old Testament stories, which Mama read to us from a large, beautifully illustrated book. She had a fondness for performance and a talent for comedy that she felt was quite acceptable in family circles but undignified outside her home. Her recitations of Paul Laurence Dunbar's "The Party" and "When Malindy Sings" or Oliver Wendell Holmes's "The Wonderful One-Horse Shay" held her four children wide-eyed with wonder.

Still, some Sunday afternoons Mama took an occasional breathing spell. Then, whoever served as babysitter that day would take us to the University of Pennsylvania Museum of Archeology or the Commercial Museum. I never tired of the Egyptian mummy display and the African and the American Indian exhibits.

We were taught pride in our family, and in the group of people known as Negroes. My father would recite the Dunbar lines "Little brown baby with sparklin' eyes, come to your pappy and sit on his knee." The love in his eyes, the expression in his voice made me feel the distinction of being a little brown baby. They read stories of the great people of the Negro race to us. Before I went to school I knew the life stories of Phillis Wheatley, Frederick Douglass, Sojourner Truth, and especially Richard Allen, the founder and first bishop of our denomination. To grow up knowing that I belonged to a wonderful race of people served to ensure self-esteem and became a bulwark against future hurt. Those formative years, without television, videos, or computers, were wonderful years that forever shaped my attitudes, values, and goals.

Newton Grammar School, a half block from my home, was integrated, as were most of the city's public schools then. Any student living within school boundaries could enroll. I was introduced to racial realities on my second day at Newton Grammar School. A little blond girl who had sought me out on opening day gave me the cold shoulder the next day. Without my asking her why,

The little Wright children. I am two and a half years old, with my baby brother Richard, age seven months, at home at 5100 Chestnut Street.

she explained that her mother said she could not play with me because I was a "nigger." My mother didn't seem surprised when I told her, but she was angry. She suggested responding with an epithet that rhymes with "rash." Still, this early introduction to racial realities did not damage my self-esteem. I always occupied seat one, row one, the position given to the person with the highest average.

I completed eight grades in six years, graduating at the top of my class. I am eternally grateful to those strict, no-nonsense teachers—all of them white—who gave me my first years of formal education. Still, they reflected the attitudes of the times. Despite my interests and scholastic standing, the counselor responsible for determining my program for the high school years placed me in the home economics course. "But," I objected, "my mother wants me in academic Latin to prepare for college." The counselor brushed me off.

That was a mistake. The next morning my mother was in the counselor's office venting a controlled but cold fury upon this benighted woman. "I don't mean to be prejudiced," the counselor declared. "There are just not any opportunities for colored girls for scholarships or for professional jobs."

"I wonder how many bright young women you've misguided because of your ignorance, prejudice, and low expectations," my mother told her. "Many of our children are lost because no parent or any knowledgeable person is there to go to bat for them."

Indeed, the low expectations most whites held for blacks came about largely because we were invisible to them. We lived in a separate world. Newspapers did not reflect our activities and achievements.

My mother's determination prevailed with the high school counselor. My roster included the complete compendium of college preparatory courses—with academic Latin. I don't believe I could have had a finer education than I received at Newton. I continued in my professional life to champion the K–8 educational model. It offers young people the stability and continuity they don't get in junior high, or "middle school" as it's called today. Too many seventh-graders experience the intermediate school as monolithic and impersonal. The differences in organization and rostering often foster poor attendance, truancy, and discipline problems. The enriched curricula that many tout as a middle-school advantage could be incorporated in the seventh and eighth grades of K–8 schools.

I received a superb, rigorous academic education at West Philadelphia High School for Girls, at that time housed in one of two imposing four-story red-brick buildings (the other was the West Philadelphia High School for Boys). I lived twelve blocks away and trudged the three-mile round trip every school day, rain or shine. Blacks represented 5 percent of the student body. Not all white students were children of privilege. Some came from working-class and immigrant homes. In those days, the legal dropout age was 14. Many children, especially boys, were forced to find low-level jobs to help support their families and never made it to high school. They could continue their education at the so-called continuation school and achieve a high school diploma.

West Philly High was blessed with a cadre of dedicated and scholarly teachers, mostly women, with degrees from Bryn Mawr, Wellesley, and the Sorbonne. I still appreciate their rigorous, unyielding approach to instruction and learning. But the place was a social desert for black students. I could get every available A and not be considered for a leadership position in the student body. One of my black schoolmates, a talented swimmer, wanted to be on the swim team. This was impossible, she was told, because the team practiced at the YMCA and blacks were not permitted to use the pool.

I had never been to Washington, D.C., and I eagerly anticipated our class trip to that city in 1926. But when a meeting was called to remind black seniors that Washington was a segregated city and we would not be allowed to stay in the same hotel as our white classmates, I decided I didn't need that trip.

Except for gym, which I hated, I was a straight-A student. English and foreign languages were my strongest subjects. I knew that the English teacher circulated my compositions among her colleagues. Yet they bestowed the English prize, awarded during the commencement ceremony, on a popular and articulate white classmate. What makes this event memorable and vivid to me even today years later, is that the department head—a very stern Miss Reinhardt who had never been my teacher—came looking for me immediately after the graduation program. "Ruth," she said, "I just want you to know that you were my choice for the English prize. I think it belongs to you." Thank you, Miss Reinhardt, even now.

As a student at a primarily white secondary school, I never had a black teacher. Much of this was deliberate, engineered by biased administrators with the cooperation of some obsequious Negroes. But the Great Migration of 1919 brought large numbers of blacks from the South to the city. They settled in North and South Philadelphia and began to enroll their children in previously or primarily white neighborhood schools. Shortly afterwards, the central administration began the process of culling and transferring white students and teachers to separate schools.

They also began to construct schools to accommodate the city's growing black enrollment. Almost overnight, spanking new schools like the Walter George Smith School opened their doors and quickly filled with black children.

George Lyle, a new black principal at the time, was told to deny neighborhood white children admission and direct them instead to the closest all-white schools. This meant real inconvenience to white parents, who were indignant over this early form of "reverse discrimination." Meanwhile, black students from integrated neighborhoods were being transferred to all-black schools like Smith. The resulting all-black schools were staffed with black graduates from Philadelphia Normal School and southern colleges. Teaching in segregated schools was often the only career available to many African American professionals at the time.

However, the black elementary schools, about twelve of them, flourished. Pupils, parents, and the community praised them for their overall excellence and commitment. Included on the teaching staffs were many dedicated professionals who did indeed produce outstanding results, as attested to, even today, by former students. They rose to the challenge and made their pupils succeed. No black teacher was assigned to teach in any school with white students. This policy was not changed until the mid-thirties, when concerted and unremitting efforts by organizations like the NAACP and the Educational Equality League forced a change.

During my senior year, ten black members of my class were summoned to the principal's office and offered the chance to attend the newly established Cheyney College for Teacher Training, a four-year school for Negroes in suburban Philadelphia. Few of us had heard of it. Most of my classmates had their sights set on attending Philadelphia Normal School, an integrated two-year teacher's college that fed the demand for teachers in the city school system. The Normal School degree did not carry the same clout as a four-year degree, but it was a sure guarantee of a teaching job. Five of my classmates went on to enroll at Cheyney.

I had been accepted at the University of Pennsylvania's fledging School of Education. My father was pleased, but I was less elated. I could look forward to another three and a half years of "integrated" education with all white instructors, except in health and physical education. Another three and a half years of being a minority student with its attendant discrimination, exclusion, and overall dullness. I had never had the joy of being taught by a member of my own race, except for the summer I took typing courses at the Duncan Business School, which was owned and operated by a black couple.

However, the one thing I learned from my kindergarten through graduate school enrollments in predominantly white schools is that intellectual acuity is not a matter of race or skin color. My success in academic competition with whites was to enhance my self-confidence and stand me in good stead the rest of my long life. I also learned that there were whites—some teachers and professors—who were fair, who were willing to see me as not just the "best colored" student they had but were able to transcend race.

When I entered the University of Pennsylvania in the fall of 1926, I was six weeks short of my sixteenth birthday, the winner of a Mayor's Scholarship and set on earning my B.S. in education. The School of Education was a new academic entity, the only undergraduate school at Penn where women could enroll.

In retrospect my university years now seem uneventful and dull. I dated moderately, socialized with my sorority sisters in Alpha Kappa Alpha, was active in church and the community. I remember how much I wanted to join friends and classmates who were eager to return to their summer jobs at fancy Catskill resorts. It seemed like a great adventure. "Daddy, please," I begged, "I would love to earn some money. Please let me go." My dad gently sat me down, saying, "Ruth, no daughter of mine will ever wait on white people." He found other employment for me. I worked as copywriter and proofreader in his office at the *Christian Recorder* during the summers.

Just as school had nurtured my intellectual development, my family had given me solid moral training. We were grounded in the Ten Commandments, the difference between right and wrong, and the principles of religion and morality. As early as age three I knew about conscience—that still small voice inside that would keep telling me I did wrong if I told a lie, even if no one else knew. We all learned the Bible verse "May the words of my mouth and the meditations of my heart be acceptable in Thy sight, my strength and my Redeemer" to remind us that foul or unbecoming language and thoughts were wrong.

Still, we never got into the morality of sex. The word was never mentioned in our home. I knew so little that I didn't ask any questions, which amazes me, since I was curious about everything. The closest I came to sex education at home was when I approached puberty and Mama did those things that mothers do, including handing me a book written for teenagers on the subject.

I recall an almost carefree teenage existence, particularly in sexual matters. The constraints were well defined and very tight. No Philadelphia high school was coeducational. The only time I saw boys was during services and youth activities at church or during visits to my father's office. Occasionally, there might be a covert exchange of glances, or some more or less flirtatious words, but it never amounted to much. We went straight home after the meetings.

Sex education in the schools was nonexistent. There was a confusing course called hygiene where we were told—it stands out clearly in my mind—that if you ate unwashed apples or peaches you could get a horrible disease called syphilis, which eventually would render you insane and blind. The teacher drew a diagram of the sex organs on the chalkboard but never mentioned sexual relations or intercourse.

When I got to college, they taught us, again during a health education class, rudimentary facts about sexual relationships. My professor emphasized the concept of "sublimation." She explained in a polite, restrained manner that we should involve ourselves vigorously in energetic and wholesome activities, sports or music or volunteer work. The idea was that if you "sublimated" yourself enough, you wouldn't have energy for activities that might damage your health and reputation and impair your educational and professional progress. There was never any mention of the word "sex."

Of course there were parties during the college years, to which I was rarely invited. When I complained about my lack of popularity, my father said, "Well, you may not have the boys buzzing all around you now, but just wait until they're ready to marry. You'll be one of the few girls they'll ask." He was right. Not that I didn't date. Of the three young men, all Penn students, whom I dated, not one ever pressured me for sex. Yes, it was a very different time, a good time in many ways.

Most of my time I spent studying hard to become a teacher of Latin and English in a Philadelphia secondary school. I was assigned to do my practice teaching at a segregated junior high school in Chester, a small blue-collar town outside Philadelphia. Twice a week, for three months, I taught Latin to ninth-grade students. It was a well-run, pleasant school, and I had no problems—except the big one: Why did I have to travel by train to another town for a required part of my degree work at Penn, when white fellow students went just a few blocks to West Philadelphia High? I had no option. There were no all-black high schools in Philadelphia at the time.

I wonder that none of us protested. Of course, we were such a minority—seven African American women in the class of 1930. Like most women of my generation, I had been reared to be "ladylike," not assertive. It never even crossed my mind to be a hero. It would be a generation before Rosa Parks would take her stand on that miserable Montgomery bus; a generation before Thurgood Marshall would lead the NAACP lawyers in the hard-won school-desegregation victory.

I graduated with a B.S. in Education in three and a half years. Barely 19, I decided to pursue a master's degree with English as my major and Latin as a minor. I had planned to take the examination for a high school teaching position until a teacher and family friend showed me a letter he had received from the personnel office of the Philadelphia School District. It read, "There is no reason to apply for a position in the secondary schools of the Philadelphia School District. At present there are no positions for colored persons."

Chapter 3

My Educational Odyssey

I CHOSE NOT TO FIGHT the discrimination and racism of the Philadelphia School District and accepted a position at Arkansas State College for Negroes in Pine Bluff. I headed south in the strictly segregated "Jim Crow car" coupled maliciously behind the train's engine. Steam and smoke blew unceasingly though the open windows of the filthy coach. Black passengers endured the twelve-hundred-mile ride with tearing eyes and soot-choked throats.

After a wretched fourteen-hour ride, I arrived in the land of Jim Crow. Leaving the train, I had begun to walk wearily into the waiting room when a porter tapped me on the arm, pointed out the "White Waiting Room" sign above the entrance, and directed me to the smaller "Colored Waiting Room." And so began my sojourn in Arkansas, a terrain and state of mind as foreign to me as Australia might have been. For two years I would live, teach, and try to adjust to the American version of apartheid. There would be no protests, no marches, no boycotts, no sit-ins, for almost another generation.

The Great Depression was affecting every region, group, and occupation. Like all other American crises, this one fell disproportionately on African Americans. Negro factory workers, always the last hired in good times, were the first fired as production slowed to a crawl. Black sharecroppers drifted north from city to city in search of a job and a breadline. Even fortunate Americans like me who managed to survive the decade between 1930 and 1940 were shaken by the misery. In rural Arkansas, the effects were devastating.

The college van picked me up that first day. As I rode the dusty back roads to the campus, I grew increasingly disheartened by the pervasive drabness of the landscape—the drooping cornfields and extensive pine forests that gave the small city of Pine Bluff its name. Four spanking new red-brick buildings stood starkly in the hot sun. A monotony of red soil, unsoftened by tree or brush, only underscored the austere and uninviting setting.

The campus was empty. I had arrived early. Most students and teachers would begin to arrive the next day. I settled into a bare but attractive corner room in the dormitory. Room and board were part of our compensation. Unmarried female teachers were housed in the women's dormitory. Young unmarried male teachers would live in the men's dormitory.

The first faculty meeting with J. B. Watson, the school's president, was imminent, and one of our colleagues had not yet appeared. People were asking, "Where is this Talmadge Hayre? Has he arrived yet?" The next morning I noticed an extremely fair-skinned young man carrying a suitcase and rushing up the sidewalk. I was about to brush by him when he agitatedly asked, "Can you tell me where the faculty meeting is? I'm Talmadge Hayre."

"Oh, they've been looking for you," I said. After I directed him, he smiled and dashed into the administration building. It was a first meeting I would never forget. Seven years later Talmadge Hayre became my husband for life.

The Arkansas State College for Negroes was more formally known, in the manner of Southern land grant colleges, as Arkansas A&M College. The *A* stood for agricultural, the *M* for mechanical, suggesting the school's mandate: to educate blacks to continue to perform manual and agricultural chores but at a somewhat elevated level. Because so much of the South's economy was still based on agriculture, it seemed important that students learn a more profitable, scientific approach to farming.

The school emphasized teacher training, too. Blacks throughout the South were in desperate need of education, and the campus included a high school for about 250 students. I had been hired to teach them English and Latin.

Many of the students were the sons and daughters of farmers and sharecroppers from towns throughout the state. The depression was cutting ever deeper, and most were desperately poor. Few arrived with dollars to pay their tuition. Many paid their way with produce or animals—cows, pigs, and chickens—that went into the college larder to feed staff and students. Some of the professionals who lived nearby sent their children to A&M's schools knowing that education there would be better than Pine Bluff's excuse for a public school. Still, no student attended without some real family sacrifice.

I really threw myself into my job. If ever there was an enthusiastic and dedicated teacher, it was little Miss Wright. I taught five English classes a day—grades nine

In the early 1930s while I was teaching in Arkansas.

through twelve, and one small Latin class. Many professional parents had insisted their children take Latin.

My students and I had a real love affair. My relative youth intrigued them; so did the distance I'd traveled, from faraway Philadelphia, and my manner of speaking. One student said, "Miss Wright, you really do talk funny." "What do you mean?" I asked. "Well, maybe funny's not the word," he said. It wasn't my accent as much as my intonation—a Philadelphia way of speaking.

I loved them. True, this was my first full-blown teaching experience, but these were truly unusual young people. Even though they were dirt-poor, these young people came to school with an ambition and motivation I have not seen since then. They had grown up on sparse farms and in sharecroppers' shacks in small Arkansas towns like Hope or Opelika, where public education for blacks was totally inadequate. What little learning they had was acquired between planting seasons, often on hard, backless benches in their country church with oil lamps for illumination and a coal stove against the chilly weather. Often, the pastor was the teacher, the Bible was the text, and instruction was minimal.

The kids I taught were the lucky ones. Their parents' vision for them extended beyond the cotton fields and cane brakes of rural Arkansas. Somehow they had found a way to send their children to this college where they could get a "real" education. I recognized and respected their almost impossible struggle for learning.

So I plunged right in and taught the high school subjects as my teachers had taught them to me. There was none of the "dumbing-down" to favor low achievers that we see now in inner-city schools. We used the state's regulation thick literature textbook, which came as a set of four, one for each high school grade. The literature included everything from Shakespeare to Conrad. No modified curriculum, no "adapted" classics, no shortcuts to learning were allowed in Miss Wright's class.

I was the stereotypical English teacher—nitpicky, precise, critical, and nagging. I had a list of "nevers" on my blackboard such as "Never say axe for ask," "mines for mine," "onliest for only," "I be for I am," "I ain't for I am not." I patiently but relentlessly corrected pronunciation and enunciation.

"I don't know if I can go around talking all proper like that, Miss Wright, 'specially when I get home. They gonna think I'm stuck up or better than them," one student confided.

"Don't worry about that, John," I said. "Just remember you are here to learn how to do things right, and it's my job to help as best I can. That's what your parents sent you here for. You must learn to speak well."

I paraded role models, great orators like Frederick Douglass, A. Philip Randolph, Dr. Watson (the president of the college), their teachers. "How far would they have gotten without the ability to speak good, acceptable English?" I asked. I was careful not to denigrate the speech of the many good, hardworking people—their parents, or even their minister—in their lives.

The battle went on for parsing, spelling, grammar, sentence structure, and paragraph building. The kids should have hated me. I did not know any better than to have high expectations and goals for them. They were struggling, long before the civil rights movement, against almost impossible odds in a racist, godforsaken section of our nation.

I threw myself into extracurricular activities, sponsoring the school newspaper and the drama club. Still, I also had a social life. The faculty was a young group, many under age 30. Our social affairs were simple affairs, Friday or Saturday night dances with the student body that strict rules governed. Faculty members were not to dance with students, a reasonable rule because the two groups were so close in age. Although students would ask us to dance, we would have to decline.

Life on the campus was pleasant and fulfilling. We often forgot that living in Arkansas was to experience the ultimate apartheid. The campus was about three miles outside Pine Bluff. I never saw whites unless I went to the town and seldom went to town except to shop. Because blacks were consigned to seats in the balcony, or "buzzard's roost," I saw no movies. Nor did I use public transportation, because I had no intention of sitting in the back of the bus.

At the end of my first teaching year, the state announced that salaries would be cut in half. The depression was taking its toll. My salary would drop from the munificent sum of $125 a month to $62.50—about $3 a day. Teachers would continue to receive room and board.

Frankly, the news didn't bother me too much, nor did it affect my interest or zeal. At the end of the two years, I had saved the impressive sum of $700, about a third of what I had earned. Of course, money went a long way then, perhaps ten times as far as it does today. That money, I decided, would be spent on a summer vacation in Europe. I arranged to travel with a friend, a former classmate at Penn.

A trip to Europe was essential, an extension of my formal education. My curiosity was insatiable. I wanted to visit the haunts of the great masters of literature I had studied—my favorites, Shakespeare, Dr. Johnson, Shelley, to name a few. I could barely wait to see France and learn more about those great writers of African heritage Alexandre Dumas *père* and *fils*. I was steeped in the Latin language. The wonders and beauties of Italy and its ancient heritage would be the capstone of my journey.

We spent four weeks in England and France and three in Italy. After the constraints of life in Arkansas, I found it a delicious joy to roam free and savor unrestricted accommodations in stores, restaurants, hotels, theaters, on buses and trolleys and trains, at drinking fountains and in restrooms. We encountered a few black expatriate Americans, especially in Paris, who were glorying in a free-wheeling egalitarian experience. We had an unforgettable time, even if we couldn't afford deluxe accommodations, restaurants, or nightclubs. Doing it so well on so little money—a grand total of $400—made me savor it more over the years!

Nevertheless, all good things end, and in September I prepared to return to Arkansas—in that Jim Crow railroad car—and begin my third year. Although I was ready for a change, no other jobs seemed available. I had applied to teach in the Washington, D.C., school system but had received no response.

When I arrived back at Arkansas State, I learned that the high school principal had left suddenly. Dr. Watson's eye fell on me, and so did the appointment. I was dubious. At age 22 I felt I lacked the experience and organizational background for the position. I had rarely paid much attention to what was going on outside my classes. Dr. Watson insisted I was the right person for the job. So I embarked on the administrative chores of rostering and scheduling, which I found difficult and wearisome. I would have been happy not to have the job. In the middle of this process, I was offered a teaching position at a newly established, all-black high school in Dayton,

Ohio, at triple my Arkansas State salary. Dr. Watson was not happy to lose me but had no means to counter the offer.

After three years in Ohio I moved to the nation's capital. The year was 1936. I had been appointed to Armstrong High, an industrial arts high school for black students whose academic potential and interest seemed limited. I found myself with youngsters who were indifferent to school—just like kids anywhere then and now. As usual, I set about energetically to change them.

In 1937 Talmadge Hayre and I were married in Washington, D.C. When we had met at Arkansas A&M seven years earlier, we had liked each other almost immediately, but I was young and not yet ready for romantic involvement. Talmadge was born near Suffolk, Virginia, the youngest son of a prosperous tobacco farmer. After graduating from Virginia Union, he had worked as a chemist—in Philadelphia, of all places—until the depression, when he was forced to join the legions of laid-off employees. He eventually landed at Arkansas State as a professor of chemistry. He was one of the kindest, most sensitive human beings I have ever known.

We had two children, Charlotte Louise, who died in infancy, and Sylvia Elizabeth, who remains the light of my life. When Talmadge was offered a position as associate professor of science at Cheyney State College in 1939, we returned to Philadelphia.

Those years away from home had helped me grow in many ways. The Great Depression had taught me that it doesn't take a lot of money to live a happy, fulfilling life. I knew I had chosen the right career. I enjoyed the never-ending challenge of the teacher's job—helping to develop a mind, change an attitude, influence behavior. My experiences validated the teachings of my youth: that no ethnic

Talmadge and I after our marriage in August 1937.

group, race, nationality, or gender has a corner on talent and intelligence.

I had learned that it is wise to take one's time before "jumping the broom" into marriage. I had enjoyed those years when I was free—to travel, to date, to enjoy the company of other men, and to practice my profession when and where I wanted. This period of freedom was precious and necessary for my personal development. My forty-year marriage would teach me that two loving, well-matched human beings can grow in maturity and understanding, and become a force of purposeful, positive energy.

Now I was returning home. I would find the racial climate had not really changed, but it would certainly seem less restrictive. I had lived and worked in the South, the Midwest, and Washington, D.C., but I always loved my hometown best. I still do.

Chapter 4

A Philadelphia Story

RETURNING HOME HAD AN ENERGIZING EFFECT. I was back where I belonged and could put down roots. I knew that the best years of my life were ahead of me. We purchased a semidetached, two-story brick house on a pleasant, tree-lined street with a friendly contingent of black neighbors. Many had young children with whom Sylvia could play, and for a couple of years I enjoyed the role of full-time wife and mother.

Then in 1940 I read that the National Teachers Examination—the first test of its kind—was scheduled for qualified candidates in the Philadelphia School District. Ten years earlier, the school district's discriminatory policies had denied me a teaching position. I was more than mildly interested in applying.

Much had changed. As the Great Depression deepened, school budgets had been slashed, and hiring was frozen. Teachers who were in place planned to stay until

In 1940 when I took the National Teachers
Examination.

retirement. Meanwhile, class sizes were growing. Young
people, black and white, armed with teaching degrees and
aspirations, were frustrated and champing at the bit.

I was more than a little nervous as I joined more than
two thousand applicants who turned out to take the
seven-hour test. I hadn't taken an examination in ten years
and had no time to prepare.

With my daughter Sylvia about 1941 on the Cheyney campus.

I scored a respectable 781 out of a possible 900. That summer I passed the qualifying tests for English and Latin teaching positions. I was set to teach in Philadelphia.

The discriminatory policies excluding blacks from secondary-school positions were no longer in effect. Beatrice Overton had made headlines in 1936 as the first black teacher appointed to an integrated secondary school in Philadelphia. Mrs. Overton had been an outstanding teacher in a K–8 segregated school, with superior gifts of personality, charm, intellect, and artistic ability. Six years later, I would join her at Sulzberger Junior High School as the second black teacher in an integrated Philadelphia school.

My appointment was made routinely, but it seemed the faculty considered it anything but conventional. I immediately sensed their barely veiled hostility. And of course the school's demographics were changing. African American families had begun to move from North Philadelphia into West Philadelphia's newer, more attractive homes. This change was reflected in enrollment.

A new junior high school, the imposing Dimner Beeber, had just been completed in the heart of white Wynnefield. This neighborhood of meticulously manicured lawns and large, graceful residences was a short bus ride away from the Sulzberger neighborhood. The white parents quietly took action. I saw gerrymandering at its best and slickest. Boundaries were changed without fuss or public debate. When September of 1942 rolled around, few if any white students were enrolled in Sulzberger. Those who had walked to school previously now took the bus. The process of deliberate and artificially induced segregation continued, an unrelenting part of Philadelphia school history.

This would be my eighth year as a teacher, and I had lost none of my zest for the profession nor my high expectations for my pupils. I had abandoned much earlier those impractical and uninspiring "method" courses Penn's professors had taught. It was obvious they had never encountered a class of teenagers. Even today, school of education graduates even at the graduate level seem to need a good amount of practical retooling and professional reshaping.

Still, for years I taught my students pretty much as I had been taught. My high school teachers had been strict, traditional, and stern, and I followed in that tradition. I had high expectations for my students and demanded their best efforts. There was not much fun, little change of pace or innovation in my classroom. Later, I realized this must have seemed insensitive to them. When I collected the Latin textbooks at the end of the term I noticed that one student had written on the flyleaf, "Miss Hayre only likes the smart ones." These simple little words jolted me. True, I did like the "smart ones." Maybe I called on them too often, praised them too lavishly, and unconsciously overlooked the less aggressive. If any of my former pupils are reading this, I apologize for what must have been pedestrian, often boring instruction. At any rate, I began to take a longer, more empathic look at students who needed more of my attention and encouragement. This lesson would be helpful when I encountered the Risers.

It bothered me that the white teachers at Sulzberger so often made disparaging remarks about the school and their students: "It's not anything like it used to be." "You can't teach 'them' anything." "I'm tired of teaching these kids—they can't learn." "I'm going to transfer where I can teach children, instead of animals." A woman actually made this last remark as she sat next to me in the teachers' lunchroom. I doubt that she anticipated my response: "The sooner you get out of these children's lives the better. It's a crime for people like you to be in the profession. Transfer today." I spoke in a level, conversational tone so as not to attract attention, but she got the message. Old and blessed with lots of seniority, she transferred without difficulty to a school of her choice. Good riddance.

Still outraged, I asked the principal for a few minutes to address the faculty at our next scheduled meeting. He had no idea what my remarks were going to be and was probably as upset as everyone else when I said, "This is my second year at Sulzberger. For seven years I've taught in schools around the country, but I've never seen the insulting condescension toward young people that I've seen here. These are good kids, bright kids, and they certainly deserve better than what they're getting here. You should be ashamed." I sat down to deafening silence. My audacity shook me, yet I felt an overwhelming sense of relief. After that, my association with old-guard faculty members was frosty at best. My friends were newly appointed black teachers, with whom I shared the same goals.

In the fall of 1945 Dr. James Duckrey, a black man, was appointed principal, another first. He had headed one of the city's all-black elementary schools. The community—parents, students, and black staff members—seemed pleased and proud to have him. But it was more than many white staff members could bear. The chair of the social studies department, a venerable soul, promptly asked for a transfer. "I just can't let my friends know that I'm working under a colored principal," she told me. This surprised me since she had always pretended to be somewhat liberal. One never knows.

I served with pride and cooperation under Dr. Duckrey's leadership. His tenure was uneventful and cautious. I remember no creative innovation or approach implemented during his term that might have rescued Sulzberger from its downward spiral. Undoubtedly, he was a great role model for teenagers, especially boys. He left after five years to accept the presidency of Cheyney.

I left Sulzberger in 1946 for William Penn High School for Girls. It was a hard-won position. Besides satisfying national and local testing requirements, applicants had to pass an oral examination before a panel of high school principals—in my case, five elderly white men. It was a daunting experience.

"Do you think a woman with a husband, a home, and a child can satisfactorily perform the duties of a teacher?" asked one white-haired man.

"Do you think that white children residing in a predominantly colored neighborhood should be required to attend their neighborhood school?"

"Would you say that kindergarten children experience any feeling of racial prejudice?"

"What adjustments should school districts make to accommodate Negroes who are coming North in great numbers? Answer these questions from an educational point of view." And even more insulting, "What would you suggest be done with unruly colored boys who terrorize white boys, stealing their books, beating them up?"

Each interviewer headed a school where no black teacher had ever taught. My guess is that each was trying to visualize me as a member of his faculty. When I left the room, I was upset. I knew that despite my best efforts I had failed.

That afternoon, quite by chance, I noticed a small article in the *Philadelphia Tribune* that mentioned Floyd

Logan and the organization he headed, the Educational Equality League. The group was new to me. I immediately called Mr. Logan and told him about the examining panel. "Perhaps I'm rushing to judgment," I said. "Maybe I should wait to see if they gave me a passing grade." Mr. Logan felt that a case should be made and immediately presented to the superintendent of schools. I composed a detailed letter describing the oral interview, pointing out the antagonistic attitudes and controversial questions unrelated to professional competence. I mentioned I was the only candidate exposed to such a line of questioning.

Mr. Logan submitted the complaint to School Superintendent Dr. Alexander J. Stoddard, who promptly called for an investigation. One examiner admitted that my interview had been unfair and that they had failed me unjustly. Dr. Stoddard ordered another oral examination and appointed two African Americans—a principal and an art supervisor—to be among the examiners.

When the names of successful applicants for senior high school positions in English were posted in the fall, I was listed number 15 out of 200. In February of 1946, I was appointed to William Penn High School, the first African American senior high school teacher in the Philadelphia public school system.

For almost forty years William Penn, an all-girls senior high school, had trained the daughters of Italian and Jewish immigrants in commercial and business education, as well as academic subjects. The school enjoyed an excellent reputation, and many families proudly counted generations of William Penn graduates. Within three years of my arrival William Penn had undergone a change. African American students were the majority, and now that the dark-skinned daughters of Southern migrants were filling the classroom seats, everything from panic to indifference was evident among the all-white staff.

In 1946, when I was appointed to William Penn High School as the first African American senior high school teacher in the Philadelphia school system. This photo was actually taken at the church where I was Sunday school superintendent.

The deliberate, systematic erosion of educational standards had grown as the enrollment of black students increased. Everywhere staff members were saying, "It's nothing like what it used to be." These sometimes subtle, sometimes blatant, always derogatory statements served to undermine the already fragile self-esteem and attitudes of their students. The principal, an aging woman who had groomed several generations of Penn students, really believed she was dealing with an inferior breed of pupil.

During my first conference with her, she told me I would teach something called Common Learnings. "I was appointed to teach English. Just what is Common Learnings?" I asked.

Father and daughter Ph.D.'s from the University of Pennsylvania. My father received his Ph.D. in 1911. It took me quite a bit longer—1949.

"Well, I'm not too sure myself," she said. "We're finding we have to do things differently." It turned out that Common Learnings was a curriculum course combining English and social studies taught for a double period. "What makes it so exciting," she gushed, "is that students determine each unit's core subject." I saw this as the beginning of the "dumbing-down" of William Penn High School and, in fact, it was the beginning of the school's academic decline.

Margaret Reed, a savvy graduate of Wellesley and the long-term vice principal, succeeded the principal. After an examination for the job, I became vice principal in 1953. The faculty received the announcement with little reaction. "My, it's really a miracle, isn't it?" said the art teacher, a woman I privately considered somewhat flaky. I had been considered an outstanding teacher since I came to the school. I also sponsored the drama club and the award-winning school newspaper. Yet none of these obvious accomplishments seemed to matter to staff members.

Two years later, when Miss Reed announced her pending retirement, she nominated me as her successor. Instead, the board named me acting principal for one full term. Then finally, in February of 1956, they made permanent the position I had literally prayed for.

I'm happy to say that this time the faculty reacted with sincere applause and congratulations. When they made the announcement in assembly, the students gave a wildly enthusiastic cheer, which quite went to my head. The Associated Press carried a story about Philadelphia's first black senior high school principal, and hundreds of telegrams, congratulatory letters, and cards and a wealth of flowers filled my office.

My appointment reflected in a small way the enormous changes happening in 1950s America. Hundreds of

In 1956, when I became the first black senior high school principal in Philadelphia. The *Philadelphia Bulletin* reporter took this picture, which I like. The picture and accompanying article received wide coverage nation-wide via the Associated Press.

thousands of black World War II veterans were enrolled in college on the GI Bill, paving the way for the extraordinary growth of the black middle class twenty years later. *Brown v. Board of Education* marked the end of legal school segregation. Rosa Parks's actions sparked the Montgomery, Alabama, bus boycotts and introduced the

Reverend Martin Luther King Jr. and other emerging heroes of the civil rights movement. Rhythm and blues, rechristened rock and roll, began to dominate the airwaves, popping up with monotonous regularity in my home and in millions of other homes where teenagers—black and white—responded to its siren song. Philadelphia, the home of Dick Clark's *American Bandstand,* became a hotbed of the new music industry until the advent of Detroit's Motown.

These were heady years. I loved my job as the principal of William Penn High. It was the peak educational experience of my life until the Risers, three decades later.

I quickly got down to business. Two things had to be immediately addressed—changes in student and teacher attitudes and a curriculum upgrade. Feelings of low self-esteem among the students were pervasive and depressing. The students didn't like themselves or their teachers. Anger sat on their faces and hostility clothed their attitudes. I would see this affliction among the Risers, three decades later. My job was to give these young women a sense of their own value, to make them feel their very real importance and see this spirit of pride reflected as they walked through the school's halls.

How to do this? I made the students partners and the chief change agents in the school's reform efforts. We asked them to devise a code of behavior that emphasized personal responsibility. Teacher attitudes were easy to influence. Most of the staff was enthusiastic and optimistic that things could and would change for the better. We became a team.

"Ruth, I've come on something that will really turn our school around," Ben Schleifer said, rushing into my office one morning. Ben, one of the most creative teachers I've ever known, was chair of the English department. He was a free spirit, well liked by faculty and students alike. Ben described a talent search program designed to encourage students to make academic strides beyond normal expectations. This unique program, originally designed for New York City students, seemed to offer exactly the elements we needed at William Penn.

With modifications as the weeks went by, we developed a program we called WINGS (Work Inspired Now Gain Strength), an acronym that Ben devised. Under Ben's enthusiastic leadership the program got off to a great start. We made it clear that WINGS was inclusive, not just for the college-bound. Each student, including those in special-education classes, embraced the program's theme, "Every girl will do her very best." The basic idea was to help every student realize she had a very worthwhile and special talent. If she could discover and work to develop that talent, she would have not only a successful school life but fulfillment as a happy and productive human being.

We had to formulate a diversified curriculum to make the program work. The traditional academic course, eliminated by the previous administration, was restored for those with the aptitude and interest needed to attend college. Students with academic majors also received supplemental reading and writing studies. Shorthand and the rigorous commercial courses, the school's former forte, were reinstated, taught by the teachers who had done such a tremendous job training secretaries in earlier years. We began to develop occupational courses for special-education students. Lucille Mitchell, a progressive and forward-looking school nurse, taught the first hospital practice course offered in the city high schools. She developed a curriculum, then transformed one big classroom into a hospital ward. The course was available not only to students considering a career in a hospital or nursing services, but also to others interested in developing additional career skills. Renee Levine, a superb teacher and former garment industry employee, taught a power machine course. We had a child development and nursery school class in which students worked with neighborhood children to learn early-childhood training skills.

I lectured the students relentlessly on the importance of knowing how to make their living in at least two honorable and productive occupations by the time they graduated. And most of our students could, when they graduated, make a living as typists (typing was a required course), clerks, secretaries, drivers, hospital attendants, child care assistants, or salespersons. The school already had an excellent home economics program under the leadership of Hazel Gray. She stressed not only the importance of homemaking skills, but their marketable aspect as well.

I tried to provide for as many students as possible a variety of experiences to enhance their self-esteem. Extracurricular activities—trips to the opera, concerts, theaters, and nearby colleges—were part of the program. We resurrected many clubs that had been in existence in the so-called good old days and created others.

None of this could have happened without our energetic, enthusiastic, and creative teachers, some of whom had replaced negative predecessors. The faculty developed a career conference, a Philadelphia first, which featured prominent speakers. In 1958, we organized a Big Sisters program, recruiting more than a hundred prominent women who were enthusiastic about mentoring our young women.

Natalie Hinderas, the internationally acclaimed concert pianist, and dancers/choreographers Carmen DeLavallade and her husband, Geoffrey Holder, performed at our assemblies. Pearl Bailey had been a William Penn student until she dropped out at age 17. I led the effort to have her visit the school. As our most famous and successful former student, she was most enthusiastically welcomed when she delivered a brief address to an assembly. Privately she had expressed a desire to receive an honorary high school diploma. This would have been a gracious gesture, but the more conservative and traditional members of the staff prevailed in their vote against presenting the degree.

Music was always an important part of our curriculum, and we had two choral groups. Several of our students went on to become outstanding concert singers. Doris Mays sang in the United States and in Europe; Bonita Glenn, a gifted soprano, achieved fame in Scandinavia; and Wilhelmina Fernandez, who starred in the motion picture *Diva*, continues to be a highly regarded concert artist.

I believe it's very important that adults—parents, teachers, principals—talk constantly with young people. We held two assemblies every week, one run by the officers of the student government association. The other was the principal's assembly, to which I invited guests or presented information I thought it was important for the students to know. I discussed behavior, stressing that two things could result in dismissal—fighting or being disrespectful to teachers. Students were told they could and would be transferred if a teacher reported back talk or rudeness. They took my suggestions well, and school life reflected their acceptance of these standards.

Society's rules about relationships and premarital sex were much stricter in the late 1950s than they are now. My advice to them, as you would expect, was to abstain from intimate sexual relationships until marriage.

The young women listened politely, occasionally with side glances and titters, but they did listen. One student said, "Dr. Hayre, I've always heard it said that if you don't have intercourse by the time you're eighteen, you'll lose your mind." I answered, "Well, I know an awful lot of women who didn't. In fact, I'm one of them, and I don't think I'm crazy."

We did have an occasional out-of-wedlock pregnancy. Usually the young woman left school, although she could return after the baby was born. In one instance we sent a teacher to the home of a senior so she could keep up with her work and graduate.

Today's horrendous truancy and absentee rates are the result of boredom and indifference. The fault for this lies with adults. If schools offer attractive inducements—interesting subjects, sports programs, enrichment activities, engaged and engaging teachers and school aides—or just an atmosphere of friendliness and security, children will respond. William Penn's attendance rate went from 72 percent up to 89 percent, which ranked us third in the city, after the all-academic Girls High and Central High Schools.

Most of our graduates found jobs after high school. And many, despite limited financial aid, enrolled in colleges. We did not have the broadscale grants and loans that are available today.

Since the 1950s, millions of dollars in tuition grants have been raised through private sources like the United Negro College Fund and our local school-based organizations such as the Hayre Scholarship Fund, the William Ross Scholarship, and the "Last Dollar" fund established by the board of education. Other benefactors have included church, sorority, and fraternity funds and a range of organizations. Federal and state financial aid programs blossomed during President Johnson's War on Poverty and the civil rights movement of the middle 1960s and continue today.

But these possibilities did not exist for our young women in the 1950s and early '60s. We did maintain a modest student assistance fund, with sums of $200 or $300 available. Small as such sums were, they could mean the difference between continuing in college and dropping out. I recall two students in particular who had to call upon the fund. One student was attending Temple University when her grandmother died. The funeral expenses depleted her savings and she had nothing left to continue her college education. When I heard about her plight, I offered her a loan through the fund, which she repaid a few years later when she was appointed a Philadelphia schoolteacher.

The other young woman went to Cheyney, did not do well, and eventually dropped out. Then one day she came to my office, saying, "I've made a terrible mistake. I want to go back and continue my education. The only job I've been able to find is washing dishes in a neighborhood dive. As I was putting my hands in and out of that dirty, greasy water, I said to myself, 'Is this all life has to hold for me? Why didn't I continue on the path Dr. Hayre put me on in college?' "

After she had unburdened herself, I offered to intervene. The college did take her back and gave her a little financial assistance. I'm happy to say that this young woman became a remarkably effective teacher in one of our inner-city schools. Recently she retired from teaching and went into the ministry.

Because of the scarcity of scholarship sources and the need for such help, I became active in establishing a grassroots scholarship fund, which would aid scores of students each year. Today more than ever our kids need that college degree, or at least some form of post–high school training, to succeed in a nation growing ever more hostile to young black people.

I did not seek publicity for our WINGS program, but word began to leak out and local reporters began to write about us. The truth of the adage that there is no more sincere flattery than imitation soon became apparent. A number of schools, elementary and senior high, initiated various kinds of programs, in many cases imitating aspects of WINGS, especially the "Motivation Program," which was developed at the senior high school.

Interest in WINGS brought many visitors to the school. One was Richard Bennett, who headed the Phoebe Haas Foundation, later known as the William Penn Foundation, one of the really great charitable Philadelphia foundations. One day he appeared, unannounced, to visit. I never asked anybody for any money—we managed with what we had—so I was startled to see him. However, I assured him he was welcome to walk about and drop in on classes. A half hour later he returned to my office.

"Dr. Hayre," he began, "the students were all in their classrooms except one young woman, who was walking a couple of hundred feet ahead of me. She saw a piece of paper on the floor, picked it up, and put it in a wastebasket." Impressed by the values and training implicit in this action, he showed his approval in a concrete way by giving $50,000, an unsolicited, unrestricted gift to help us further our program. In 1960, $50,000 went a long way— chorus uniforms, an organ, acquisitions for our art collection, tickets to cultural events, and much else. I had to add to my repertoire of homilies, "You never know who's watching."

Our teachers continued to be great boosters. They went forth with good news about the school, its students and programs, and the innovative things they were doing to upgrade the program. The staff deserves accolades because of their extraordinary performance, wonderful creativity, and unflagging spirit of cooperation. I cannot praise highly enough their faith in and dedication to their students, their devotion to high academic achievement, and their ability to transcend the school's racially phobic past. They were unhesitatingly willing to move the program along in a myriad of ways, from writing the school show to escorting students to an evening performance of *La Bohème.*

The reactions of the students to their school were overwhelmingly positive. They respected and honored their teachers and looked upon me as a strict and demanding mother who loved them—as I told them so frequently in assemblies. Most of them were proud of their school and were careful to refrain from bad behavior. One student was quoted to me as saying, "Dr. Hayre may smile a lot, but don't mess with her."

Over the years I have run into former students on the street, on the bus, in a school, or at a reunion. They invariably greet me with overwhelming warmth and big hugs and kisses. One middle-aged woman I met recently proclaimed to all who would listen, "You're the best principal I ever had! God bless you." What a reward!

By the time I began my fifth year as principal, I was receiving widespread recognition and had been nominated for several awards. But the best commendation I received came from my teenage daughter, who was attending a suburban high school at the time. We had moved to Cheyney's suburbs to be closer to my husband's job. After attending one of our school shows, Sylvia said, "You know, Mom, I wish I were at William Penn. You seem to have so much more good stuff going on, trips to the opera and that kind of thing. We don't have these activities at our school at all." I had vowed when I took over the principalship that I would make William Penn the kind of high school I would want my daughter to attend. It seemed I had accomplished that mission.

Chapter 5

The Climb to the Boardroom

I N THE SUMMER OF 1963 I took the next turn in my educational odyssey. I had been at William Penn for eight years when I was appointed superintendent of District Four, the largest and most complex of the city's eight school districts.

The civil rights movement was making big waves. And in Philadelphia, the demands for improving city schools were becoming increasingly insistent. As I sat mulling over the calendar on my second day in office, a short, stocky, and very angry man brushed past my secretary. He shouted, "We're going to picket Allison School. We've had enough of these inferior, broken-down buildings which are not fit for our children. We're going to do something about it. We have a hundred people picketing. You better get over there."

71

At Sylvia's graduation from Oberlin in 1963, the year I took the next step in my educational odyssey when I was appointed superintendent of District Four. That was truly a momentous year. Talmadge and I were proud parents.

I arrived at an exceedingly dilapidated building. The structure was crumbling. Inside the building a white powder, apparently asbestos, flaked the floors. There were no indoor toilets, children had to be escorted to outdoor facilities. I was shocked. "You're absolutely right," I told the irate parents. "I don't know how you put up with this. Give me a picket sign. I'll get in line." The children were temporarily transferred to other buildings, and within a year a fine new structure had replaced the school.

During my first few weeks as District Four superintendent, truculent community leaders demanded the removal of principals in three North Philadelphia schools. These situations were satisfactorily resolved. However, one school, Simon Gratz, continued to come under severe community criticism. Over the years I had watched with dismay as Gratz, once an excellent high school, accelerated its downward slide. This deterioration was the result of staff attitudes similar to those I'd encountered during my early years at William Penn.

Gratz's former vice principal had succeeded the retired principal. When I met with him I asked, "Have you had a chance to set your goals? What improvements do you have in mind?" He looked at me as if I were crazy and said, "Well, no, I've been on vacation. I haven't had a chance to think about what I'm going to do." Now, he was not new to the school. He should have known exactly where he wanted to begin. I calmly suggested, "We're both new and I've thought of some goals I'd like to see carried out in the district. I'm sure we'd both like to see a high degree of academic achievement and a significant improvement in attendance and retention rates." He could barely conceal his amusement.

I left Gratz determined to stop that kind of indifferent, uncommitted administration. Mary James, the president of the home and school association, was an invaluable ally. A vocal, aggressive community activist, she made it clear that the Gratz community wanted the new principal out. Period.

Mary James plunged right in, bringing her very vocal constituents into play. They demanded a new principal. Her activist pressure permitted me to have a frank discussion with the principal and his eight department heads. I solicited their suggestions for the academic program. I tried to ease their hostility by telling them that community leaders were pushing me, too. Those two hours were as tense a session as I've ever experienced. They repeated the litany of tired clichés still in use today: "You can't expect anything better of students who come out of such straitened circumstances. We can't change their environment or their poverty." This language is always used to excuse the absence of aggressive educational leadership. It masks the refusal to set goals or accept professional accountability. At this point in the meeting it was growing dark and no one had suggested turning on the lights. "Gentlemen," I said in closing, "the hour is late, the sun has set, and darkness is approaching. This is the situation at Gratz as well."

I was determined that the school would not continue its slide. No school can be better than its leader. The principal began to realize his situation was untenable. After a few visits from Mrs. James and her parental cohort, coupled with official reaction to a detailed report I'd sent downtown, he was reassigned to a position at the board's central administration office.

Who would be the new principal? I called Marcus Foster, an energetic young educator. "Marcus, do you have your secondary-school principal's certificate yet?" I asked him. "Because I have a job for you." I'd known him for a long time and planned to recommend him for the Gratz principalship. He had been my husband's student at Cheyney, where he regularly fell asleep in class. Talmadge didn't take it personally. He knew Marcus was bright and was working nights to make tuition payments.

Marcus went on to become principal of an elementary school, where he distinguished himself by creating a fine motivational program. He adapted that program to use at his next post, a disciplinary school for special-education students, where it was hugely successful. I knew his talents and commitment could resurrect Gratz High School. I assured Mrs. James, who had not heard of him, that she would be very happy with the choice. They became great allies in the crusade to turn the school around.

With Marcus Foster. I prize this photograph, taken when Marcus was still the principal of Gratz High.

Marcus was an effective and visible leader, mentor, and role model for twenty-five hundred young people at Gratz High School. He spurred them on to academic achievement and improved attitudes and behavior. His success in reviving a rundown, depressed, and ineffective high school became front-page news. In three years Marcus Foster became the city's most outstanding educator.

Eventually Marcus accepted the superintendency of the Oakland, California, school district, where he again became a shining light. In this highly visible position he was a target of the lethal Symbionese Liberation Army and was assassinated as he was leaving work one evening. Bob Blackburn, his top aide, was seriously wounded. I miss Marcus to this day. What a tragic loss!

During my first few years as district superintendent, I wanted what most people want—to be well thought of by my colleagues, the district principals. A modus operandi where we could work as a team, where I wouldn't be perceived as the "enemy," had been my goal. I soon realized my chances of popularity were slim. I could not smile and be sweet. These fellows had to be made to do the job they were hired for.

Parents and community leaders were agitating for more community control and involvement. We established a community advisory council and organized PEP, Parents for Educational Progress, a district-wide parents' movement to increase parental responsibility. Once the district became decentralized, I immediately attacked the reading problem. We initiated a guaranteed-performance reading program from the Behaviorial Research Laboratories for grades one through three. Test scores reflected a definite improvement after the first year. We initiated three magnet programs—academic, art, and music—that proved highly effective in attracting and keeping able high school students.

I cannot write about my tenure during the turbulent '60s and '70s without some reference to the mercurial, controversial Mark Shedd, who became superintendent of schools in 1967. Shedd's educational innovations included intensive involvement of community advisers, classrooms without walls, television teaching, and a degree of decentralization that made each of the city's eight school districts practically autonomous.

During this period the spirit of black revolution was pervasive. Students demanded black history courses, the right to display the African black, red, and green flag alongside Old Glory, and other "relevant" items. The dispute I remember most vividly occurred at the board of education building on May 17, 1970. On that day thousands of students left their high schools and marched to the central administration building in an orderly fashion. The po-

This is the picture I like best. It was taken when I visited the Ethel Allen School in 1969. I am surrounded by three groups of third-grade pupils and three happy teachers.

lice commissioner, Frank Rizzo, ordered two busloads of police, fully equipped with guns and clubs, to the scene. When the students arrived, a small group was admitted to meet with the superintendent and appropriate parties. The rest of the teenagers milled about outside in reasonably good order until Rizzo ordered the police to disperse the crowd. Children were beaten with police clubs. Others fled. Those who refused to disperse were taken to police headquarters, where they were held without being charged. When Rizzo became mayor, he promptly fired Dr. Shedd.

Many people saw the student demonstration as characteristic of the Shedd administration—uncontrolled, without focus or positive result. Dr. Shedd was sincere on issues of diversity and innovative programming. He was a risk-taker committed to making a positive difference. However, I believe his tenure would have been quite different had he focused more on instruction and carefully considered educational objectives, especially student achievement. He died in 1991 and left many friends who continue to sing his praises.

During these years black pupil population was increasing quickly, and frightened whites were fleeing to the suburbs. My job included reminding principals and teachers that I would not tolerate any lowering of standards or expectations just because there was a change in complexion.

The strong emergence of the teachers' union as an aggressive and often hostile organization has made a long-term impact on education. There is no question that teachers need a union. Teachers endured abuses for years. Women were paid less than men, hours were sometimes unreasonably long. Faculty meetings were an excuse for a domineering principal to harass the staff. I know this from personal experience.

The teachers' union was originally mandated to protect teacher's rights and assure good wages and favorable working conditions. However, union representatives sometimes exceeded their directives. They encouraged strikes and insisted on protecting marginally effective—often incompetent—teachers. These two developments were a waste of educational opportunity for all children.

Today, union and administration are learning to work for the good of children and the welfare of teachers. After all, if it were not for the children, there would be no jobs to protect. It might be helpful if more people would remember this before they begin blaming the victims—children—for adult failures.

Groundbreaking for Edward Heston School during my term as district superintendent.

I supposed I must have done something right during my twelve years in District Four when more than twelve hundred people bought tickets to the retirement party held in my honor. The proceeds became the beginning of the Ruth W. Hayre Scholarship Fund. Today, the fund enjoys the support of parents, teachers, and a range of benefactors. In the eighteen years since its inception, it has grown into one of the largest scholarship funds in the city and served as a model for at least six other funds. To date, more than twelve hundred students have received more than $1 million in tuition expenses.

After my retirement in 1976, the District Four superintendency was assumed by Dr. Jeanette Brewer, an exceptional young administrator. I was delighted to see her appointment to what would become more than a decade of service to our children. I left knowing that the district would be in good hands.

I began a happy and full retirement, traveling, playing duplicate bridge, painting, reading, and taking my two grandchildren on the occasional trip to Disney World. I did accept a job as adjunct professor at the University of Pennsylvania Graduate School of Education, but it was short-lived. Perhaps it had been initiated at too advanced an age. By 1981, I felt I was finally done with the educational bureaucracy.

I was wrong, and not for the last time.

I kept abreast of what was happening to the public schools. The news was appalling: declining test scores, uncaring teachers, uninterested students. No one was addressing these problems, certainly not the school board. When a nationwide search was initiated for a new superintendent of schools and I was asked to consult, I suggested it was time for a woman superintendent. I felt that no one could be better suited for the position than Dr. Constance E. Clayton, a product of the city schools, a lifelong educator and administrator right here in the Philadelphia system. The committee agreed and appointed her to an outpouring of accolades and acclamation.

Dr. Clayton had a daunting and backbreaking job. Schools had been racked with frequent and long strikes;

teachers were disgruntled and demoralized. Fiscal management had been poor. Parents regarded the school system with pessimism and distrust. Dr. Clayton did not let any grass grow under her feet. Working with parents, teachers, and administrators, she developed a standardized curriculum for kindergarten through twelfth grade. She began a wave of reform in many areas. Among her innovations were magnet school programs, desegregation programs, Paths-Prisms, and similar programs. For all eleven years of her tenure, the school district was free of labor unrest, and for the first time in many years the schools were financially sound. Philadelphia citizens, including a large cadre of businessmen, became strong supporters of the schools. There was a widespread feeling of trust, confidence, and admiration for this superintendent.

Dr. Clayton's experience as superintendent was totally positive. Schoolchildren called her "Miss Connie." Her motto, "The children come first," became a rallying cry for Philadelphia's educational efforts and was imitated in other cities. Adults accepted and revered her.

My desire to ensure that she had at least one firm friend on the board led me back to the school system. Dr. Clayton encouraged my interest in a seat on the board, the mayor approved, and in due time they appointed me.

I soon found Dr. Clayton didn't need any help from me. She worked hard and supervised a tight ship. I felt her program was so excellent and her administration so sound and effective there was no reason for major complaint. Dr. Clayton retired in 1993 after the longest tenure of any large-city superintendent. In December 1990, I was persuaded by Mayor Wilson Goode with the board's overwhelming backing to accept its presidency—the first woman to head the board of education in its 118-year history.

On the occasion of my election to the Philadelphia Board of Education in 1990. With me are (from left to right) Constance Clayton, board vice president Andrew Farnese, and Senator Vince Fumo.

I had barely sat down in the president's seat before I was faced with a critical issue. A thin, intense young man rushed to the front of the room, shaking a finger at me and demanding that the board of education respond to the terrible danger AIDS represented by putting condoms in the schools. Other advocates lined the walls at the back of the room, and began throwing condoms and comments. Some landed on the board table where we were sitting. I was flabbergasted and totally taken aback, but displayed neither emotion.

I could not ignore the school system's responsibility for AIDS. The state has always mandated and stressed the importance of abstinence as part of sex education. However, increasing numbers of young women were becoming pregnant before marriage. The incidence of sexually transmitted diseases was increasing. With the advent of the deadly AIDS, it seemed criminal to withhold facts and services that might help save our teenage population. Not having a carefully planned curriculum to address AIDS and the burgeoning phenomenon of teen pregnancy seemed ridiculous. The board set up a carefully selected task force on teenage sexuality that included two of the AIDS protesters. The task force recommended that the senior high school sex education curriculum include instruction on the value and the use of condoms in preventing teenage pregnancy and the spread of HIV and AIDS.

They further recommended—and this step was pushed by ACT UP—that condoms be distributed in every high school. ACT UP members themselves threatened to distribute them outside the high schools. Their opponents, particularly a group known as the Family Life Organization, a far-right religious group, plagued the board meetings and me personally for many months to defeat the proposed policy.

Inviting correspondence from all six (formerly eight) districts, the board received an avalanche of mail. The vote was roughly fifty-fifty. And the board was divided along the same ratios. The controversy was personally distasteful to me, a clergyman's daughter raised with moral constraints. Yet I knew that given the grave danger the AIDS virus presented to sexually active teens, I had to take action. If it would save the life of even one student, it would be well worth the effort and the public criticism.

The board of education finally came up with an excellent statement. The policy reaffirmed our stand that abstinence was the best method for preventing teen pregnancy and sexually transmitted diseases. However, the

Here I am holding up a condom given to me by a member of ACT UP as I talk to the press about the distribution of condoms in the schools.

board recognized that there should be some provision for services, specifically the availability of condoms, to those students who would not accept the idea of abstinence. The use of condoms would be taught in the sex education courses.

Two key points in the policy probably were responsible for its citywide acceptance. The taxpayers' money was safe; condoms would not be paid for from the school district budget. Parental involvement was sought, with every parent having the right to veto—in writing—a child's participation in the condom-availability program.

And so I reach the end of my formal educational odyssey. The journey has been endlessly fascinating—sometimes frustrating and wearisome but always rich in psychic rewards. My life has been inspired by children, beginning with those depression-era students in Arkansas. Those practically penniless sons and daughters of black sharecroppers came to that Arkansas college in search of education with little more than grit and mother wit. All of them went on to become good citizens and some to become distinguished leaders.

I have found my greatest satisfaction in the modest role I played in helping realize that transition. I have seen how a person can defy the circumstances of birth, race, and social class to make a positive contribution in life—and how a person born with some small privilege can help others find their way up.

I often reflect upon the lasting impact on me of that little black boy who was the most disadvantaged person I have ever known, my grandfather Richard Wright. Born a slave, he made himself into an icon of optimism, hope, trust, and faith with the simple statement: "Sir, tell them we are rising." I could try to do no less. This is what gave me confidence to move on to the next, and most exciting, stop in my educational odyssey.

Chapter 6

Not What We Give but What We Share

IN 1987 I WAS 77 YEARS OLD. I had decided to let my hair go gray. Although I was still active in the world, I was beginning to consider my mortality. How could I make my remaining years exciting and involved, yet different from my earlier experiences?

Money was not a problem. Over the years, the combined income my husband and I enjoyed had given us a good life while we were healthy enough to enjoy it. While our lifestyle was not expansive, neither was it penurious. We had danced in the streets of Paris on Bastille Day, climbed the pyramids of Egypt and Mexico, walked the Great Wall of China, and floated in dhows on the Ganges and steamers on the Amazon, Mississippi, and Danube. In the process, we had smelled not only the roses, but many an orchid. Our travels had been joyous and extensive before Alzheimer's (his) and knee replacement (mine) cruelly curtailed our wanderlust. We had managed the requisite two cars, our daughter's college education and wedding expenses, reasonable charitable contributions, modest entertaining expenses, and just plain good times.

When I received a lump-sum annuity upon my retirement, however, I decided to splurge. I purchased a Lincoln Continental Town Car, a 2 1/2-carat diamond ring, and a mink coat. By this time, my dear husband's illness had progressed to the point that he could not assess my actions and therefore gave no comment. He benefited from the Lincoln for the remaining two years of his life when we drove on family visits and vacations to Cleveland, Boston, Washington, D.C., and Virginia.

After suffering for years from Alzheimer's disease, Talmadge died in 1977. Always financially judicious, he left a respectable estate. These monies, added to my assets, would easily carry me through the next twenty or thirty years, including the possibility of nursing home care. I enjoyed an adequate pension and Social Security benefits that were enough to live on. I sold our suburban home and purchased a center-city condominium. As a financially independent widow, I had sufficient means to live out a comfortable old age, provided I stayed away from scams, unwise investments, and a second husband.

Still, I longed for something more challenging, something new and different in my life—something that transcended the comfort of the rocking chair.

In 1981, I read about Eugene Lang's "I Have A Dream" Foundation, which promised to pay the college tuition for sixty New York City sixth-graders, predominantly Hispanic and black, when they graduated from high school. A rather neat idea, I thought.

The program's originality and possibilities for motivating poor, inner-city pupils fascinated me. The idea that I might do something similar never crossed my mind. Where would I ever get that kind of money? Yet, a few years later, I found my net worth had almost tripled since my husband's death. In ten years, I had grown from "comfortable" to almost wealthy. I had far more money than I needed for my remaining years.

Quite candidly, Reaganomics made this possible. I knew that once elected, Ronald Reagan would introduce an income tax reduction plan that would benefit his friends, millionaires in the 73 percent tax bracket. I was in the 48 percent bracket, and while I didn't find it really burdensome, I was not pleased with that amount of payout. Sure enough, after the election my taxes were reduced and I·found myself in a newly defined 28 percent bracket. Moreover, all kinds of loopholes were available to the wealthy—for example, limited partnerships with heavy write-offs. I invested in a few. They eventually failed, taking my money with them, but in the process allowed me to recoup just about all the losses in tax write-offs. This type of deal no longer exists, but stories of millionaires who didn't pay a dollar in income tax were common during the eighties.

Moreover, the Reagan years brought an astounding rise in interest rates for certificates of deposit, bank notes, and municipal tax-free bonds. Interest rates on home mortgages were at an all-time low. In the late seventies I took out a 7.5 percent mortgage on my condominium after being advised that the balance could be invested at 9 percent, 10 percent, even eventually as high as 17 percent. (This last figure was from a local bank on a ten-year note. No wonder it went out of business!)

My assets had grown, almost without my notice, until it dawned on me in the fall of 1987 that I had more money than I would spend in my remaining years. If I died the next day, the government would claim a huge amount in inheritance taxes.

My life span was becoming shorter, its tenure ever more fragile. I could not leave this earth knowing I had not shared the wealth that God had blessed me with. I have often quoted the poet James Russell Lowell, "Not what we give, but what we share, for the gift without the giver is bare." The idea of "giving back" became almost an obsession. I wanted to share in some small way the lives of those who would receive my help.

How could I best use the money to help my fellow human beings? Should I target the needs of the homeless, the jobless, the incurably or mentally ill, the incarcerated, the undereducated? Whatever pebble I might throw into this vast ocean of despair would not make the slightest ripple. Still, children, helplessly caught in the vortex of these often hopeless conditions, needed all the help they might get.

I did not take long to decide that I would invest in the lives of economically disadvantaged children. I had followed the Lang program with interest over the years. Now I felt financially able to follow suit. But could I deal with the physical and emotional demands involved in relating to scores of adolescents? Despite such misgivings, I took the plunge.

I called Mr. Lang's office and several days later received material about his program. It included the project's history, a delineation of goals, implementation procedures, and application forms for individuals or organizations with $250,000 who would like to set up an affiliated program. After thinking about it for several days, I decided the "I Have A Dream" Foundation was not for me.

To my surprise, Mr. Lang called several days later encouraging me to become part of his organization. I said I had read his material with interest and appreciation but had decided on a different course. I didn't want the constraints of personally administering his tight, very well structured program. I hoped to affiliate with a Philadelphia university that would accept the idea, handle the money, and provide some facilities as well as a substantial research component.

I mentioned that "I Have A Dream" was a good inspirational name but I had another, more personally meaningful name in mind: "Tell Them We Are Rising." I thanked him for providing the model that had stimulated similar philanthropical programs for poor students.

Then I approached Dr. Constance Clayton, Philadelphia's superintendent of schools. I held her in high regard and wanted her opinion. Her reaction was enthusiastic and immediate. She pointed to her brown arm to suggest that, racially, my gift would represent a philanthropic milestone. (Bill Cosby had not yet donated $20 million to Spelman College.) Still, I could sense her surprise. I told her I imagined other friends and acquaintances would have reactions that ranged from "Poor soul, has she lost it?" or "How on earth did she get that kind of money?" to "What some people will do for attention!"

I would have preferred to give anonymously, but Dr. Clayton insisted, "No, it's important that blacks let their benefactions be widely known. We need examples in giving and philanthropy." I had to agree. With my permission, Dr. Clayton consulted Rosemarie Greco, the president of Fidelity Bank and a former board colleague, who graciously dispatched two members of her staff, a vice president and a financial adviser, to check out my financial condition. I guess I might have been offended at what some might see as an invasion of privacy or as intellectual condescension, but I wasn't. Connie and Rosemarie were good friends and I knew they wanted to protect my interests. I placed my books on the dining table. After they had examined everything, the vice president looked at me with new respect, saying, "I only wish you could teach me how to save money."

Temple University had agreed to facilitate the program. I was delighted. President Peter Liacouras's enthusiasm was obvious from the moment we began to discuss the Riser program and its possibilities. We were to enjoy a productive relationship for the next six years. After an investment strategy meeting with the university's financial officers, I felt assured that my contribution would effectively maximize over the next six years. Meanwhile, it was safely salted away in the college's coffers. Each year they have provided me with a financial report. Our formal agreement, drawn up by the university's legal counsel and vetted by the school district counsel, was clear-cut and fairly simple. It ensured that my donation could not be touched for six years, when they would disburse funds to cover tuition costs for those Risers admitted to college or some other post–high school educational program.

These grants would be supplemental based on other financial aid or grants available to the student. However, the promise was clear: No eligible student should have to pay a dime of tuition, but I would not supply room and board for students who chose a college away from home.

Temple, under the auspices of its College of Education and with oversight provided by Dean Richard Englert, would act as liaison between the program and the university. They would guide and assist a full-time coordinator, providing part-time administrative services and generous access to the university's physical facilities.

Mrs. Deloris James, a seasoned community and school leader, was selected as program coordinator. Her job was clear-cut: to keep in touch with 116 youngsters; encourage parental participation, maintain student files on school achievement and attendance; arrange and keep records of interviews, home visits, and background meetings with counselors and health personnel; and gather any other pertinent information.

We were ready.

Chapter 7

The Leap of Faith

N OW, WHO WOULD BE THE RECIPIENTS, the "lucky" children? I sought no advice. This decision would be mine. I had two firm requirements—poverty and a North Philadelphia address. How many kids should I select? Should I seek out students whose attendance, grades, test scores, and family stability indicated they would be the most successful? Or should I just go ahead and choose two sixth-grade classes at random? I decided on the latter course.

The sixth-grade class of Wright Elementary School was almost a preordained choice. Not only did it meet the criteria, but the school was named for my grandfather. I chose the second class from Kenderton Elementary School, some three miles away. Why did I pick Kenderton out of the region's twenty-three schools? The principal's dedication and competence impressed me, and I thought it might prove an extra advantage to her pupils.

Let me make something clear: I am not naive. This program was no altruistic exercise on my part. My motivation stemmed in part from an intellectual curiosity born out of a life spent in education. I wanted to know to what extent this kind of intervention would alter the "predictable" path of at least half of my kids. "Predictable" in the language of social scientists and educators refers to the tools used to define and measure potential scholastic success or failure in the 1990s—pupil attendance, standardized test scores, behavior, parental involvement, dropout rate, and academic success by subject grades.

By these standards, at least half of my 116 students were seriously at risk by seventh grade, when I chose them. Fifty to 85 percent of my Risers would drop out of school between ninth and twelfth grade. Forty percent were likely to be truant on any given day. One-third would commit some kind of disciplinary infraction, anything from general unruliness and disorder in class to serious incidents such as bringing drugs or lethal weapons to school or assaulting a teacher or student. Only one out of ten ninth-graders would continue on to some form of higher education. Obviously this last statistic was the one I most hoped to alter.

I asked for and received the graduate lists of both schools. I also requested final grades, standardized test scores in reading and math, percentile ratings, parents' names, and, when possible, approximate family income and any indication about welfare status.

Most of the students came from single-parent homes, family incomes were incredibly small, and often the grandmother was head of the household. Although a few Kenderton students were reading above grade level, at least half were below grade level. Math was pretty much the same story.

Information on the Wright School students was almost a mirror image of Kenderton except that twenty-seven of the sixty-four graduates were classified as special-education students. Of these, ten were classified L.D., or learning disabled—not severely retarded but deficient in reading and math skills. Tests had determined that at least eight were classified as E.M.R. or T.M.R., educational or trainable mentally retarded. They would continue to receive instruction adapted to their individual needs and attend classes of no more than twelve students. Another six were found to be S.E.D., socially and emotionally disturbed. These pupils must be tested also, but they are usually identified as severe behavior problems—hyperactive or destructive children. All except the learning disabled may remain in school until age 21, when they qualify to receive a Supplemental Social Security stipend. Most of the Risers in this category did not graduate. Their parents wanted them to stay in school until they were 21.

So these were the figures on my Risers. These youngsters to whom I was to commit much of my life for the next six years were very much "kids at risk." I was not fainthearted or despairing. Nobody had told me this "leap of faith" would be easy.

The day before the graduation, I asked the school board driver to take me through the Riser neighborhoods. I had served this community as teacher, principal, and district superintendent. I had traveled North Philadelphia streets visiting schools and attending community and church meetings, block parties, and demonstrations for thirty years.

Was it my imagination, or did the streets and houses seem more rundown than two decades earlier? The flight

The way things look in the areas surrounding the places where some of my kids live. Fortunately, most lived in areas that looked better than this.

of capital and jobs has left North Philadelphia, once a bustling center of commerce, largely bereft of employment possibilities. It is the city's hardest hit and most poorly served community. There is no neighborhood library, recreation center, or playground.

We made our way through narrow one-way streets lined with two- and three-story brick row houses, some shabby, others well kept, all still sporting the architectural embellishments popular at the turn of the century. Graffiti screamed from many walls, vacant lots filled with household discards and broken glass were an eyesore, but there were also spots of positive brightness. A large shopping mall faces Wright School. One of the shops, a sporting

goods store, is owned by Juanita Norwood, who would become an adopter of the school. A new health center, a church, and a senior center are in close proximity. As we drove through the neighborhood, children, from toddlers to teenagers, filled the streets, jumping rope, playing games, and shooting hoops as adults caught a breeze and chitchat on front steps.

Most neighborhood families live in blocks of tidy, well-kept, beautifully appointed brick row houses on tiny side streets off Ridge Avenue. One street is notable for the exquisite wrought iron doors that front each home. On another, tires retrofitted with a profusion of colorful, cascading plants brightly announce each address, testifying to the liveliness and longevity of the city's block committees. The next block shows a communal face through its uniform, freshly painted blue and white homes. Turning the corner I encountered the mural of a fantastic Eden rising above an actual garden of collards, lettuce, tomatoes, and other comestibles. This last, a reclaimed former vacant lot, is sponsored by the Philadelphia Green Association, an agency that supports neighborhood garden clubs. Yet even in these residential blocks the occasional boarded and vacant house stands as spoiler, a constant irritant to residents who work so hard to improve their surroundings.

My newly minted seventh-graders would be leaving elementary schools in close-knit neighborhoods like this to attend larger, stranger, more distant middle schools. Many Kenderton pupils would join seventh-graders from five other elementary schools at Gillespie Middle School. Wright students, depending on their addresses, would attend FitzSimons or Strawberry Mansion Middle School. FitzSimons boasted several noted alumni, among them Bill Cosby and a former board of education president. For years, the school had been a hotbed of faculty dissension, and I shuddered as I contemplated the two-year sojourn my Risers would spend there.

A handful of Risers, twelve to be exact, would be enrolled at Strawberry Mansion Middle School, a sprawling red-brick complex made up of three educational units: Hill Elementary School, Strawberry Mansion Middle School, and Strawberry Mansion High School. Some children go from kindergarten to high school graduation without ever leaving the corner of 32d Street and Ridge Avenue, often called "The Ridge," just one block east of the entrance to Fairmount Park, with its tennis courts, the Robin Hood Dell open-air concert facility, and a children's playground within easy access.

As its name suggests, Ridge Avenue is a main route, the spine, so to speak, of the Risers' North Philadelphia.

Its diagonal path provides a shortcut to downtown Philadelphia. It is a struggling community and one where the children have hopes so high and dreams so big that I could only pray the schools, and my program, would supply some foundation to support both.

I wondered how many children attending Strawberry Mansion have been told of the role their school played in cracking the wall of union bias against black construction workers. In fact, how many teachers and other staff members know that hundreds of blacks, led by Cecil B. Moore, a lawyer and president of the local NAACP, demonstrated on the site, waving signs and shouting slogans to block all work—even lying down in the street defying bulldozers to run over them? This riveting confrontation ended after the NAACP called on blacks to vote against the $15-million school bond issue unless the board of education guaranteed nondiscrimination at all its building projects. This threat brought all parties to the table, and shortly afterwards, the first black construction workers walked on the site in triumph.

Farther down The Ridge other businesses, greengrocers and ubiquitous mom and pop stores purveying both candy and high-octane malt liquors, fight to hold off the encroachments of vacant lots and boarded-up buildings. The mouthwatering smells of barbecued chicken and pork drift from steel drums and barrels. Close by, a portrait by a neighborhood artist depicts a beloved retired policeman and the fruit-and-fish stand he formerly owned. The scene is lively, if unduly populated by idle youngsters who should be in school. I would discover later that the car wash doing a brisk business helped supplement the sparse family incomes of some of the Risers. Houses where the underground economy—gambling, dope, and prostitution—flourishes are only a sidestreet away.

Although Ridge Avenue and its surrounding blocks were home to half my kids, the other half, those from Kenderton, were clustered in Tioga, an area farther north. They lived in many of the three-story structures built at the turn of the century by the well-to-do whites who wanted a residence near prestigious North Broad Street. When the owners left for more attractive areas in the suburbs, they became absentee landlords, cutting their fine houses into tiny apartments. What were once fine one-family dwellings became multifamily misery. During the '70s and '80s, many families with their children would move as their buildings became uninhabitable.

These are the neighborhoods surrounding the middle schools many Risers would attend. Later we would consider the "comprehensive" or "neighborhood" senior high schools, Gratz and Strawberry Mansion High.

Actually there was no mandate for any Philadelphia student to attend a neighborhood school. Risers who qualified might attend one of the more innovative and culturally diverse magnet schools. At least 20 percent of Philadelphia's 256 schools could be rated excellent to outstanding. The better schools are the magnet schools, academic high schools or schools in the "desegregated" northeast area of Philadelphia. Many of the magnet schools were developed to promote some kind of desegregation by attracting white students to schools with specialized programs. Many of the spaces in the program were reserved "for whites only." Only blacks with high academic achievement, high scores on standardized tests, and impeccable attendance and behavior records would be admitted, unless they knew a board member or a politician or had a really savvy parent who understood how to work the system. This was the physical, emotional, and academic terrain the Risers would negotiate during their middle-school years.

Nobody had told me this leap of faith would be easy. This challenge was just one of many I had experienced over my long life. I had taught, counseled, and loved young people from many different parts of the United States. The vast majority, poor and black, had overcome the odds against them. True, this job would call for more strategies and resources than I had needed before. These were the 1980s, an era with different mores, dangers, and certainly a different social climate.

I knew there were many skeptics who would scoff at my idea that a promise and a program could alter the destinies of these children. Yet if my forebear Richard Wright had heeded similar "facts" about his chances in life, would he have walked two hundred miles for an education, headed a college, founded a bank? I could not give up on children who might in other circumstances have been mine. Rising? Yes, that seemed the way to go.

Tomorrow would be graduation day. I began my trip home.

The school district had arranged an eight a.m. press conference to be held at Temple University on June 24, 1988. From there we would go to graduation ceremonies at Kenderton and Wright Schools, where "Tell Them We Are Rising" would be announced to parents and students for the first time.

The school district's press release had described only the program and the cost involved. Curiosity about the identity of the "philanthropist" had been rife for several days. A perceptive friend, a local reporter, had called me two days earlier to ask, "Do you have any idea who it is? Could it be Jim Wade or maybe Julius Erving? Bill Cosby, perhaps?"

I was appropriately vague and noncommittal. I was taken aback by his persistent conjecture and intense curiosity when he called again the next evening. Finally, in a tone that smacked of suspicion, he said, "We have been assuming that the donor is a black man, but now it's being said that it's a woman." "Could be," I answered innocently. "Wish I knew. Anyway, they'll make the announcement at tomorrow's press conference."

The next morning reporters, columnists, television cameramen, and anchors filled the Temple conference room. My friend the inquisitive reporter was among them. I can only say that his face was a study in puzzlement when the official announcement confirmed his suspicions.

On graduation day I saw my sixth-graders for the first time, and all doubts fell away. I was overwhelmed by the sense of caring, of high hopes and responsibility I felt. Suddenly here were Mequaya, Tamika, N'Kechi, Kilea, Tamla, Taneema, and Mieshia—faces to go with those enthrallingly musical names I had seen on paper. Here were Rasheed, Tzar, Jawaan, Khalil, and Hakim along with the traditional Roberts, Jameses, Wendells, Edwards, and Tyrones. Although we had not met, I knew their goals. Several weeks earlier, I requested that their teachers ask each student to write a composition on "My Goal in Life." They produced carefully crafted statements concerning their dreams and aspirations. I was impressed.

The girls were resplendent in a wide variety of styles—strapless dresses, for those with enough bosom to hold them up, bouffant taffetas, form-fitting satin, full-skirted cottons. The boys, not to be overshadowed, were elegant in pale-gray tails or white tuxedos; others settled for the impeccable business suit. Such elegance was not unusual at many sixth-grade inner-city graduations. Although I secretly yearned for the traditional cap and gown, this tangible evidence of the love, affection, and pride of caring parents—or an aunt or grandmom at this event of a lifetime—warmed my heart.

There, in front of the students, parents, and faculty and under the glare of the television cameras, I made the announcement that would change our lives—the students' and mine—for the next six years:

> I, Ruth W. Hayre, have given a sum of money to Temple University, in the care of Dr. Peter Liacouras, President, and Dr. Richard Englert, Dean of the College of Education, to be set aside and invested so that the initial amount will appreciate after six years. At that time, the funds shall be used almost exclusively to provide tuition assistance for each student in the June 1988 graduating class of the Richard R. Wright School. Each student will be accepted into an accredited college or other post–high school program. Funds will be available for four years or as long as the student remains enrolled, not to exceed four years. This means that any and every member of this class can go forward to finish high school, and seek a college education with full tuition paid.

The Risers were seated behind me, and I couldn't see their immediate reactions in the overwhelming tumult from parents, friends, teachers, and press. Later, viewing the video, I was struck by the surprised, uncomprehending response of the students. Most, I think, had little or no understanding of the announcement's importance. How could a little girl whose first bra was pinching her, or a little boy anxious about the fit of his pants, get excited about something this old lady was offering six years into the future?

"College? Never really thought about it," responded 12-year-old Johnnie Crawford, when a reporter solicited his comment.

On that day in June 1988 I couldn't foresee that in this group of 116 small, shining faces and great expectations, sixteen would drop out, one would die from accidental food choking, three would be incarcerated for petty crimes and incorrigibility, two would be arrested, tried, and found not guilty, and twenty-two would become unwed mothers.

But on that morning, as I watched the children in their graduation finery, I only envisioned the positive things—high school graduation, good behavior, and no run-ins with the law.

Thank God, this was true for most of them.

Chapter 8

Getting to Know You

THE DOOR OPENED. Kathy, a small and delicate girl, entered.

"Weren't you one of the graduation speakers at Kenderton last year?" I asked.

"Yes," she replied, beaming at the recognition.

"Well, how do you like your new school? And what do you think of the Risers program?" I continued.

"It will pay my way to college," she said.

"Not all of it," I corrected, "but it will pay your tuition, the largest expense. Have you thought that far ahead?"

"Yes, I want to be an engineer."

"Great! This is a good report card. If you continue getting grades like this, you'll make it." Again, she beamed. Our ten minutes were up. I gave Kathy a hug, and Mrs. James took our picture. I was encouraged by our meeting and engaged by her lovely, responsive manner.

Kathy would earn consistently good grades throughout high school and enroll in Drexel University.

⌢

Jack lumbered in and approached the table. By far the largest boy in the group, he must have weighed over 250 pounds. I searched for an icebreaker, then noticed his resplendent, immaculately white sneakers. "What great sneakers," I ventured. A broad smile immediately transformed his face. However, "uh-huh" or "okay" was his only response to any other conversation I tried to initiate. He wasn't impolite, just not ready to open up.

This same taciturn Jack would develop into a "smart mouth." He was on the verge of suspension when we met again at Germantown High School a few years later. A Japanese throwing star—a sharp, six-pointed device—had been found hidden in his shoe during a routine weapons sweep. "Mrs. Hayre," he explained with a straight face, "I don't know how that thing got in my shoe. I was walking along, minding my business, when somehow it must have stuck to my shoe."

"Jack, it was inside your shoe. How did it get there?"

"You know, I've been trying to figure that out," he replied, still deadpan. I dropped the subject. I was afraid I would explode with laughter—a totally inappropriate response. Because Jack had no prior incidents of bad behavior, he got off with a reprimand. But by the time he reached his junior year, it was clear that his academic performance left a lot to be desired. Jack had passed only two subjects.

"Well, I can see you have no interest in finishing high school," I said when we met again. "You have four credits when you should have eleven. You've shown no improvement."

And then the floodgates opened.

"Mrs. Hayre, nothing's gonna keep me from graduating from high school. I may not graduate on time with the rest of the group, but I'm gonna get my high school diploma," he proclaimed emphatically.

Jack then began to denounce the principal, loudly and clearly. I stopped him. "Don't blame the principal or anybody else for your own laziness."

"Okay, Mrs. Hayre," he said quietly.

He transferred to William Penn High School, now coeducational. He did graduate, a year behind his class, and enrolled at Philadelphia Community College.

The Risers' introduction to middle school began with the misplaced records and staff shortages that are constants in every transitional semester. But the program was in place. Deloris James and I began regular meetings with Temple's support to smooth out glitches and fine-tune the program. Mentors who would serve as friends and counselors were beginning to meet their charges

I could have quietly withdrawn and left the children to be tended by the project administrator, the mentors, and Temple University for the next six years, but such a hands-off approach didn't suit me. Given what I knew of the odds, I couldn't imagine the Risers struggling to meet the scholastic demands my gift entailed without some assistance from me. After all, wasn't I frequently quoting Lowell's "It's not what we give, but what we share, for the gift without the giver is bare"?

The children had responded to my greetings and hugs with shy smiles on graduation day, and I'd been touched by their vulnerability and youth. I wanted a one-to-one ongoing relationship with each child. They were 12 years

Meeting with two Risers in the ninth grade at Girls High.

old. I was 78. Was I too old to bridge our generational gap? We had grown up in radically different times and circumstances. Yet we shared racial and cultural bonds and aspirations for the good life.

I decided that my role would be to cheerlead and guide them through the thickets of education—three years in the confusing shoals of middle school and three more in high school lay ahead. Our relationship had just begun. I would begin by meeting each Riser after the first middle-school report cards were issued. We would discuss each pupil's expectations and any difficulties he or she might be having.

They say God doesn't make mistakes, and so I must believe that he put me in the position of second grand-mother to these children for a reason. Surely he knew how little prepared I was to confront their turbulent lives, despite my fifty-plus years in education. At-risk children comprised a substantial percentage of the 116 Risers; barriers of poverty, violence, and abuse informed the geography of their lives. I learned about their aspirations, frustrations, and troubles firsthand. I observed at close range the bewilderment, pain, and deep-welled hostility that neither they nor I could entirely understand, nor could the Riser structure of parents, mentors, and teachers always remedy. And as much as I thought I knew, I learned even more. I can't say how grateful I am to have been even a small part of their lives.

Deloris James arranged our meetings at Gillespie Middle School, where most former Kenderton students were enrolled. I planned to speak with each of the twenty-four students, and I allotted ten minutes for each meeting. The time might seem brief, but it would allow us the up-close and personal meeting I wanted. I aimed to get a sense of each student's interests and concerns, and I hoped they would begin to know me as someone other than a name, or face, in a newspaper article.

Eighteen of Gillespie's twenty-four Risers were in school that first day. The six absentees, it developed, were already on the road to dropping out. The Risers waited in the outer office, in groups of six. Because it took a good deal of logistics to arrange these meetings without interfering with major course work, we would do it no more than three times a year.

The principal, who had volunteered his office for these meetings, greeted me warmly and ushered me in. I came armed with a computer printout of Riser report cards and a box of candy bars, one for each student. I sat down somewhat nervously and waited for the first student to enter.

This is a Saturday morning tutoring session in math, with Alma Crocker in charge.

Angela had been a good student during elementary school, but I noted two failures, in math and English, on her first report at Gillespie.

"Hello, Angela, what a pretty necklace!" I enthused.

"Yes, ma'am, thank you. My grandmom gave it to me for Christmas."

"How do you like your new school?" I asked.

"I think I liked it better at Kenderton. But it's okay."

"Angela, you seem to be having problems with math and English. In middle school you must pass all your subjects or you'll have to repeat the whole grade. And I know you are a good student." Her lovely face took on a worried, or somewhat puzzled, expression, as she acquiesed with a "Yes, ma'am."

Three months after that first meeting, I noted she was failing the same two subjects. I went back, in what would become my modus operandi, to check on students with failing grades.

I sensed Angela's anxiety and immediately addressed the repeat failures in math and English. "Have you talked this over with the teachers?"

"Yes, sort of."

"I just don't understand this. I know you're a really good student."

"Well, I don't always understand the math even though Ms. Kelly gives me makeup homework on the days that I miss class."

"You have an excellent attendance record. How do you miss class?"

Then came the unbelievable explanation. She participated in a volunteer program at Widener, a school for physically handicapped children with deeply serious needs. Though barely 13, Angela had somehow been recruited, and had become a committed, dedicated helper. Three days a week at eleven o'clock, the school van transported Angela and three other students to Widener, a mile away, where they "worked" until one o'clock. Her duties consisted of helping the younger children with lunch and rolling wheelchair-bound pupils to class. It was clear that this activity meant a great deal to her.

"But, Angela, if you are gone from eleven to one you miss two of your most important classes."

"Oh, it's only for three days a week, and the teachers make sure I have the homework."

"Do you understand how to do the math homework?" I pressed her, but got no answers.

Angela was clearly distressed, and I promised to look into the matter. "I don't want to see you fail at the end of seventh grade."

I was seething. How dare the school mess up a child's academic progress in this way? True, the experience was commendable, but idiotically scheduled. The principal pleaded ignorance. "You're right, Dr. Hayre. I'll look into it."

The school's solution was another example of the ineptness that seems endemic to middle schools. They decided to take Angela out of the program entirely. Why couldn't they have rescheduled the difficult classes for the three morning periods? That way she could have continued doing something she really loved and was good at.

Angela went downhill. She didn't pass math or English, nor did she try to. She had to repeat the entire seventh grade, including subjects she had successfully passed.

She made it to senior high, one year behind the Risers. Then Angela began to have trouble with her mother. When she was 16 she became pregnant and her mother put her out of the house. Both the mentor and Mrs. James did all they could to help and reclaim her, but to no avail. Angela, who was underage, dropped out and became a nude dancer in a North Philadelphia go-go bar.

Not all the Risers I met that first day were receptive to my attempt to develop a relationship. Danyelle had an excellent scholastic record. She came in with a smiling countenance and greeted Mrs. James and me politely.

"Danyelle, I see you are really doing well. All A's and B's and no absences," I said happily. "What do you think of the Risers program so far?"

"I'm happy to be part of it. I've always wanted to go to college, and this makes it possible," she answered in a calm, measured, and mature manner.

I made a couple of other inquiries in an effort to get to know her. But she was and would always be reserved, at least with me. I rarely saw Danyelle after that.

She had little interest in the Riser activities, or in her mentor. Danyelle's mother was pleasant and cooperative and kept in touch. Danyelle completed high school, was admitted to Penn State University, and thus could claim the Risers' tuition promise.

Van introduced himself with a cheerful "Hi" as he entered the office. A small, wiry child with a mischievous smile, he moved with a certain assurance. A fair student at his elementary school, Van received similar marks on his first report card at Gillespie. We had a small discussion prompted by the '76ers tee shirt he was wearing. "It's not hard to guess your favorite sport," I said.

"Oh yes, basketball. I play a lot of it," a statement that gave me pause since he was so short. He played in Police Athletic League games.

Van became quite attached to me in those early years. He was the Riser chosen to appear on my eightieth birthday video. He also appears posed with his thin arm encircling my shoulder in a group photo illustrating an article on the Risers published in *Ebony* magazine.

Although I felt Van had the ability to do well, he was not an academic achiever. He slipped easily into ennui. Many of his peers showed the same lack of motivation. Our frequent meetings had little impact on his academic performance.

At one point he was picked up with three other young boys on charges of car theft. He and Mrs. James persuaded the judge that he was an innocent bystander, and I believe he was. Van fell out with his mentor, who became disenchanted because Van would not "toe the line." Although I no longer talked with Van regularly, I was encouraging whenever I saw him. He responded in kind, but I had my doubts.

When most of his classmates were in their senior year, Van had an eleventh-grade classification. Then somehow Van got a shot of motivation and turned over a new leaf. It may have been the help of Mrs. Farmbry, the principal. But I think a surge of peer pressure, the positive kind, inspired him to move ahead. He saw his best friends—outstanding basketball and football athletes, whom he worshiped, and others he recognized to be on the right track—leaving him in June for college or other interesting places.

In an uncharacteristic burst of energy, he managed to pass most of his eleventh-grade classes and enrolled in summer school to earn the credits he needed for promotion into twelfth grade. He graduated a year behind his class and joined the U.S. Marine Corps, following in the footsteps of his good friend James. I have heard nothing of him since.

I was able to complete fifteen interviews that day. I was just too tired to continue and returned two days later to conclude the meetings. The next week I visited FitzSimons Middle School, where thirty Risers were enrolled, and then finally Strawberry Mansion Middle School for additional meetings. The rest of the Risers had chosen to at-

Meeting with Riser Gary Wall, a student at Gratz High.

tend parochial and public schools in other sections of the city.

Gradually a feeling of trust began to develop between me and the children. As they matured and experienced more problems, they often contacted me at home. One evening Jesse, a small, quiet boy, called. "Dr. Hayre, I'm calling you to let you know I'm quitting. Nobody cares anything about me at that school." Jesse was classified as a special-education student because his emotional problems apparently could not be handled in regular class.

"But Jesse, what about your counselor?"

"I don't have one," was the response, often true, that I'd heard from several Risers.

"Well, Jesse, whatever you do, stay in school. I'll see what Mrs. James and I can do."

Our efforts were unsuccessful. Eventually Jesse threatened suicide and was sent by his distraught grandmother to live with an uncle in North Carolina, where we hope he continued his schooling with appropriate guidance and help.

One night Analie called, in great distress. "Dr. Hayre, I don't know what to do. I have nowhere to go." I could hear a baby screaming in the background as I asked where she was calling from.

"I'm staying with my girlfriend."

"Surely you can stay for the night, and I'll speak to your family tomorrow."

The next morning I called the mother at her job and the grandparents at home. Although this very stable family previously doted on Analie, they had practically thrown her out when she became an unwed mother.

With intervention from many people—her mentor, her counselor, the principal, Mrs. James, and myself—her situation was resolved. Although Analie's grandparents were working, they gave mother and child a home. After much prodding, the Gratz day-care center found a space for her child. Analie was back on the school rolls, vowing that she would graduate with her class in June despite all the obstacles. She did just that, nothing short of a miracle.

During her senior year, Marcine, one of our most promising students, involved me in her college plans when she announced she planned to study journalism at Point Park College in Pittsburgh. She had heard vague reports about the school and seemed determined to attend. In fact, she was accepted by the time I heard about it.

I was somewhat upset with her choice. She had attended no career-counseling sessions and had received no direction about selecting a college. "Marcine, I have never heard of this place," I said at our next session.

"I read about it in one of the college booklets and sent off for their catalog. I'm sure I'll like it."

"But how much does it cost?"

"Something like seven thousand dollars for tuition and three thousand for room and board."

"How do you plan to pay room and board? The Riser scholarship doesn't cover that," I reminded her.

"Oh, I have that taken care of; my family will pay for the room and board."

"And have you thought about additional expenses—transportation, phone—that you would have to pay being away from home? Besides, what's wrong with Temple? It has one of the best journalism departments in the country." I named some of the successful print and television journalists who were Temple graduates. To no avail.

To make a long story short, she did go to Point Park. Mrs. James soon began to hear rumors that Marcine was unhappy with her choice. As it happened, I had a school board conference to attend in Pittsburgh. When I learned that the college was only five blocks from my hotel, my ever-present curiosity got the best of me. I called the college, spoke to a very surprised Marcine—and paid her a visit the next day.

The college was situated in downtown Pittsburgh, right in the middle of the same kind of inner-city environment she'd left. A drab building, a twenty-story renovated hotel, served as a college. Everything—classrooms, dorms, and business office—was housed in this building, which stood starkly on a bedraggled, seedy street, with not even one tree to improve the landscape.

Marcine received me enthusiastically and gave me a tour of the college, which did not take long. She finally stopped in the dorm room that she shared with another student. "Yes, Dr. Hayre, I made a mistake. I should have listened to you."

Academically she was doing well, she explained. She really liked her teachers and the course work. Later, I learned that Point Park has an excellent reputation as a school for communications.

"But Dr. Hayre, there's nothing to do here," she continued. "I can't go out because the neighborhood is dangerous. I don't have any friends. There are no sororities. And the boys!" She rolled her eyes and sighed hopelessly.

There was also a big bill for room and board hanging over her head. I advised her to take out a student loan since she hadn't been able to come up with the money. But the long and short of it was, "I want to transfer to Temple for the spring term." Because of her good grades we were able to engineer her acceptance at Temple, where she is on the dean's list.

We were midway through the school year when I met with Nate, a tall, slim, very solemn young man, just past his thirteenth birthday. I called his attention to two failures. "How could you fail social studies?" I asked. "That always seemed like an easy subject to me."

"Miss Hayre," he began, "she flunked us all. She said she wouldn't pass us because we were just a bunch of dumb niggers." I couldn't believe what I was hearing, nor could I believe the calm, resigned composure of this child.

"Did you tell your mother?"

"No, I never bother her with school stuff. Miss Hayre, the kids do act bad. They don't listen to her." A pause. "They even call her names."

"Like what?" I urged. He was reluctant to repeat the words. "Go ahead. It's okay. I think I should know."

"Real bad names, Miss Hayre, like m——f——," he said, abbreviating the word, "bitch, dumb broad."

I asked the principal to check out what might develop into an explosive situation. He informed me that the teacher was indeed incompetent, unable to control her classes, and resorted to racial epithets out of sheer frustration.

"What about Nate?" I asked. "Here's a good kid who's the victim of this teacher's ineptness. I insist that you find some way to give Nate and other students a chance to pass this seventh-grade social studies."

The teacher was transferred to another school, the district's classic way of dealing with unsatisfactory teachers. And Nate did pass social studies and was promoted.

The Risers Club met Saturday mornings at Temple facilities. The first hour was usually devoted to math and English tutorials by the city's master teachers. A foundation grant covered these costs. The attending Risers voted it one of the best parts of the program.

The rest of the morning was used to plan future activities. Ron James, the group clubleader, and whoever served as the elected president of the Risers Club managed these sessions. I attended as an observer.

The Risers made group trips to the Afro-American Historical and Cultural Museum, Penn's Landing, the city's

Emma Chappell, founder of the United Bank. Risers visited the bank and opened up accounts.

waterfront entertainment area, the renowned black theater company known as The Freedom Theater, and Temple University. Often family members and mentors joined in these excursions.

I personally importuned U.S. Congressman William H. Gray III, at that time the third-ranking official in the Democratic House, to invite the Risers to the Capitol as his special guests. A Bell Telephone official, Charlie Green, donated the money for buses. The trip was free to all Risers. Parents and mentors were welcome. It was requested that they pay a small fee. Preparations were intense. Coordination, scheduling, and discussions about appropriate attire and protocol generated great and growing excitement.

Risers with Joan Harris, mentor, in Washington, D.C., when we visited Congressman Gray. It certainly seems as if Joan is keeping all the boys happy.

Seventy-nine people signed up, mostly Risers. I was somewhat disappointed when only sixty-one showed up. But we had a great time. The children were well behaved and smartly turned out in brand-new white tee shirts emblazoned with "Risers" in bright turquoise lettering. From their seats in the visitors' balcony, they listened briefly but with interest to congressional speeches before lunching in one of the congressional dining rooms as Congressman Gray's guests. Later they were photographed with him on the steps of the Capitol building.

A similar trip was planned in the fall. This time the twenty-five Risers spent the weekend at Fellowship Farm in Bucks County, forty miles north of Philadelphia. This impressive rural retreat was a spinoff of Fellowship House, nationally known for its influential endeavors in human and race relations. The newly constructed buildings provided very attractive facilities for retreats and small conferences. The bucolic setting, the peace and quiet of the countryside that seemed to stretch for miles and miles, would be a decided contrast to the sights and sounds of city neighborhoods.

The program had been carefully planned with the help of the Farm's highly skilled professional staff, who were familiar with interests and needs of inner-city kids. The weekend's activities emphasized self-esteem, self-actualization, motivation, trust, getting along with people, and "beating the odds." Every Riser present was ready to brave this new experience.

The children left Philadelphia early on a Friday morning after a careful briefing about behavior and overall expectations. They were accompanied by four familiar and well-liked adults. By ten-thirty, they were settled in and beginning their first session. I was impressed with the tailor-made program of activities generated by the Farm's staff.

The morning session was led by a vibrant young African American man. He had arranged the Risers in a circle and was plying them with questions: "Who am I anyway?" "Who are you?" "Do we trust each other?" These exercises were interspersed with games in interpersonal relationships and self-awareness. There was lots of hand raising and involved activity. Children who usually were noncommittal were participating with unaccustomed verve and energy.

By the time the session ended and lunch was announced, the atmosphere was relaxed and happy; the children were enjoying themselves and felt at home.

All but one. Tanita was still unhappy about being at the Farm. As we walked to the lunch building she said, "I don't want to stay. I don't like it here."

"But what do you dislike?" I asked. "Everyone else seems to be having a good time."

She kept repeating she didn't like it. She wanted to go back to the city with me, but I told her that couldn't be done without parental permission.

"I don't know these girls. They act like they don't want me here," she insisted.

"Well, Tanita, since we can't do anything about it, why don't you try being a good sport and make the best of it? Now put on a bright smile for me." After more coaxing, she changed her attitude. She had a good time.

After a great lunch, which included homegrown vegetables and homemade apple pie, I returned to Philadelphia, but not until each Riser had given me a hug, a ritual I had instituted early in our relationship. Often our children grow up cold and unloving because demonstrations of affection are not a regular part of their lives. I believe the hugs brought them closer to me, and me to them.

They spent the afternoon swimming, playing games, and hiking. After dinner, Deloris James and Joan Harris, one of our most effective mentors, called a meeting of the girls, which lasted most of the night. Deloris called the activity a "social workshop." They gathered in the big living room adjacent to the dormitory where the girls would sleep five to a room with a sixth bed for the adult supervisor, Deloris James, Joan Harris, or Gladys James, Ron's wife (neither is related to our coordinator).

Deloris James particularly wanted to reach four girls who were discipline problems. They had been allowed to come on the trip with the hope they might benefit from it and not spoil it for others. Deloris James had her antenna out for indications of possible trouble.

During the course of the evening the girls discussed how to get along with one another, especially in close quarters, and away from home. They noted that often people, especially teenagers, get into fights, sometimes deadly ones, over nothing. "Stuff like he-say, she-say, or I don't like that look you gave me, or she thinks she's better than me," volunteered Katina, and everyone agreed. Others volunteered observations of their own.

"Sometimes a girl with pretty hair and nice skin will be beaten up by other girls," one said.

"Just jealous," another girl explained.

"People like lie just to start a fight," another chimed in.

"You're right. Someone told me she heard I was after Georgie, the boy Ron James brought as a guest. They said me and him were going to the woods after everyone was asleep. Now you *know*, Mrs. James, I would never do anything that crazy." Robina was almost too emphatic in her declaration of total innocence.

But Deloris James was relieved. Robina had recently spent a year in a disciplinary school for girls because of her inability to stay out of fights. Yet on this occasion she did more to befriend Tanita, the reluctant Riser, and bring her into the group than anyone else.

"We have to learn how to like one another and help one another," one Riser said in summation. Deloris James felt that something important had been accomplished in building trust and understanding among her charges.

The next day, after a morning and afternoon of workshops, food, and recreation, the Risers returned to Philadelphia. Quite happily, it seems.

The most successful and best-attended convocations took place three times a year—mid-October, Valentine's Day, and Recognition Day at the end of the school year. We convened in the Temple University Health Center, and divided into three groups—Risers, mentors, and parents. For one hour each group discussed their specific concerns and agendas before reconvening for the day's program presentation.

The programs were dictated by Riser interests. Conflict resolution, teen pregnancy, relationships, sexuality, black history, career workshops, drug abuse, SAT workshops, and self-esteem were among the topics addressed. Speakers who were experts in the subject area addressed Riser interests and concerns. We found that what turned some kids on left others unmoved. As the students matured, they became more vocal and participatory.

Chapter 9

The Mentors

The strong, capable, and ambitious leave the inner city. The next generation remains behind—without mentors. The challenge for today's mentor is to reach the soul of the promising but neglected youngster who sees no way out of poverty. Mentors seem to relate naturally to others; they project something akin to love in their willingness to commit to another human being, at the same time there is a certain reserve in the relationship.

Margaret Mahoney, *Mentors*

THERE IS NOTHING NEW ABOUT MENTORING. It goes back as far as ancient Greece and has antecedents in the Old Testament stories of Moses and Joshua. Soon after my decision to "adopt" 116 preteens, I began to consider how I might build psychological supports for the children. As the fall semester approached I was feeling more and more like the old woman who lived in a shoe. The number of

129

children in "Tell Them We Are Rising" far exceeded those in similar programs.

Over the next six years, my 12-year-olds would become young men and women. They would begin to experience adult interests and urges without the attendant maturity, experience, and responsibility. Of course, they would continue to have many adults in their lives—parents, counselors, teachers. But, unfortunately, there are parents who do not, or cannot, parent, counselors who do not counsel, and teachers who do not teach. This is a reality. I have seen many children fall through the cracks because they had no one to catch them.

Each Riser would need a one-on-one relationship with a caring adult who would be a friend, confidant, and companion on our social and cultural outings and would also keep a weather eye on school progress, attendance, and behavior. Where could I find mentors who met the criteria Margaret Mahoney prescribed?

During the original Risers press conference, I had asked for interested volunteers to serve as mentors. More than two dozen men and women representing a range of racial, religious, and economic backgrounds responded. I also received a call from Richard Tyre, who represented the Uncommon Individual Foundation. Tyre trained mentors for business and corporate outreach programs. Although his training program had not involved adolescents, he wanted to give it a try. When I told him we had no money to pay for his services, he said, "Oh, I'll do it on a volunteer basis." Richard Tyre became our primary trainer for the mentoring program and a great and good friend as well.

I needed about one hundred mentors. Where to find them? I didn't have the resources for television advertising that organizations like Big Brothers and Big Sisters employ in soliciting mentors. Then I thought of my sorors, the members of Alpha Kappa Alpha, the oldest black sorority in the nation. Although a full dues-paying member, I was only semiactive in the Philadelphia chapter. I maneuvered my way onto the agenda of the next meeting and made my pitch before one hundred fifty of my sisters.

I must have been reasonably eloquent and effective, because fifty women volunteered. The truth is, I really begged. I have no idea whether the members offered their help out of friendship or because they viewed the program as an interesting challenge, a way to give back to society. I really worked the "give back" concept throughout my appeal.

Well, now, I thought, that takes care of the girls. Now what about my fifty-five young African American males, soon to face the pressures, hazards, and temptations of adolescence? Help! I cried.

And fate, in her more beneficent aspect, intervened. I was to receive an "outstanding citizenship" award during the Founders' Day celebration of the Mu Omega chapter of Omega Psi Phi fraternity. Their members turned out in significant numbers, and I spoke to them of the strength, power, and potential commitment their organization represented. I addressed their ability to make a real difference in the lives of young people, especially our boys. Certainly Omega Psi Phi's social, cultural, and fund-raising activities were commendable, I said. Yet much of who they were—their essence—was going to waste unless they reached out to help those who desperately needed the human gifts the brothers had to give. "Thank you, gentlemen, for this award," I concluded.

Certain that I had not influenced anyone, I was surprised and grateful when a distinguished gray-haired man who introduced himself as A. J. Wells said he was not only

Omega Psi Phi mentor with Risers at the fraternity house for a Saturday afternoon tutoring session.

willing to join my efforts but would use his influence to have his brothers become part of the mentors program.

He was true to his word. Many of our mentors came from Mu Omega's ranks. The fraternity was extraordinarily supportive and generous. It sponsored two always much-anticipated annual events—the Riser Christmas party and a summer barbecue on the lawn of the fraternity house. The influence of Wells and his community-minded men, all role models and mentors for our boys, cannot be over-estimated.

And so my group of mentors had formed themselves. The initial group of 123 were unusual for their diversity. They ranged in age from 25 (a recent Princeton graduate) to 81 (a retired teacher). One hundred twelve of the mentors were African American, eleven were white. They represented a spectrum of occupations—clerical worker, veterinarian, educational consultant, former school administrator, physician, public relations consultant, social worker, and secretary. They shared a common commitment to improving the lives of young people.

We accepted everyone who volunteered, giving little thought to anyone's credentials for what would turn out to be a rugged job.

How did we match mentor and child? Scientific methodology was not our rule of thumb. We didn't know enough about the Risers to say, "Here's a good kid certain to succeed" or "This one might be a troublemaker." We didn't want to be accused of stacking the deck. We made our matches by lottery.

The fledgling seventh-graders gathered at FitzSimons Middle School where they would meet their mentors, who, it is no exaggeration to say, were champing at the bit. Boys' names were placed in one box, girls' names in another. After picking a name, the adults located their mentees and spent fifteen minutes getting acquainted. Then each member of a duo was asked to introduce the other to the group, each telling what they'd learned about the other. It was an enjoyable and effective exercise.

The concept and responsibilities of mentoring had been explained to pupils, parents, mentors, and counselors earlier. Richard Tyre shared his definition of the true nature of mentoring:

> Any and all relationships that provide a brain to pick, a kick in the pants, and someone who'll listen are "mentor-rich atmospheres." Mentors perform the delicate contradictory roles of supporting and pushing. This requires a *mutually* affectionate, trusting relationship. It takes time and is rare. When it occurs, it is—after family and love—the most powerful relationship for changing human behavior.

Tyre's sessions were eminently practical and down-to-earth. I especially like his Ten Commandments of Mentoring:

1. Thou shalt not play God.
2. Thou shalt not play teacher.
3. Thou shalt not play mother or father.
4. Thou shalt not lie with your body language.
5. Active listening is holy time and thou shalt be non-judgmental in your listening.
6. Thou shalt not do for someone what they can do for themselves.
7. Thou shalt not lose heart because of repeated disappointments.
8. Thou shalt be aware that some people move in straight lines, others in fuzzy curves. Everyone is different. Thy protégé is not thy clone.
9. Thou shalt not believe thou can move mountains.
10. Thou shalt not desire thy neighbor's protégé, nor thy neighbor's success.

Needless to say, these commandments were broken as often as the ones Moses brought down the mountain. Still, they were a valuable guide.

How did this diverse group work out? The stories, like all human experience, are cautionary, celebratory, and often a mixture of both.

Riser Johnny Smith is the youngest of five children. His mother is Jewish, with the characteristics often associated with Jewish mothers—protective, ambitious for her children, and demanding. I wish all our parents had these traits.

Mrs. Smith had insisted that Johnny did not need a mentor. She and his father had set goals for him and did not need an outsider in their plans. Because she was trying hard to protect him from bad street influences and negative peer pressure, she preferred he not attend Riser meetings or events. In other words, "Thanks, but no thanks."

Johnny managed to survive the two years of middle school, where so many of his fellow Risers met failure and defeat. He kept out of fights, got along with his teachers, and avoided suspension. His academic record was commendable, though not brilliant, and he was accepted to Bodine, the city's high school for international affairs. Bodine, one of the city's magnet schools, was set up to encourage white parents to send their children into black neighborhoods, to further so-called desegregation. The magnet schools are small compared with the comprehensive neighborhood high schools. And the black students who are admitted have fine academic records and demonstrate good behavior and attendance.

Most parents whose children attend magnet high schools are pleased. I am sure Johnny's mother maneuvered and fought to have her son accepted to a magnet school. Johnny did well at first, achieving a B average. Then his mother died suddenly. I didn't find out for weeks. I doubt that Johnny talked about it, and I'm sure his father was too shocked to discuss it.

His third report card showed a marked decline in grades—C's and at least two failures. Teachers complained that Johnny was just "fooling around," not taking his work seriously. It seemed obvious he was having difficulty dealing with his mother's death. His former elementary school principal, Dr. Edna McCrae, tried to counsel him. Then she suggested that we assign a mentor. His father, still in shock and unable to continue the strong parenting his wife had provided, agreed.

Dr. Raymond Ragland, a black physician and Omega Psi Phi member, enthusiastically agreed to serve as Johnny's mentor. The father of two teenage sons, Dr. Ragland welcomed Johnny into the family almost as another son. Johnny never missed a Risers event—a meeting, a party, a trip, an Omega cookout—and his mentor was almost always there. During his junior and senior years, he was seen almost exclusively with a very attractive young woman, whom he brought to most of the Riser events. I never had a chance to talk with her, but I'm sure his mentor had the appropriate discussions with him.

After ninth grade Johnny transferred from the magnet school to Gratz, his neighborhood high school. His mother would not have been pleased. But the young man had the good sense to know what he really wanted most could not be found at Bodine. He had a consuming interest in playing varsity-level football and baseball and hoped to be good enough to earn a football scholarship. His mentor advised him that a clean life was a prerequisite to athletic success—no drugs, alcohol, or cigarettes, and preferably no sex, but if it had to be, make it safe sex.

Johnny threw himself into the life at Gratz, at least the athletic aspects. His grades, however, were mediocre. When I talked to him about his academic failures, he was his usual charming, cheerful self. "Don't worry, Grandmom. My teachers say if I make up certain assignments, I can pass." I reminded him of the school board's policy— two year-end failures and you are off the team for the next year, or until the failures are made up.

"Don't worry," he repeated. "You know I'm gonna get a football scholarship to Syracuse University."

"Great, I hope you do," I said. "I'll have to pay less money for your tuition. Do you know that Syracuse also wants a 1000 score on the SATs?"

"I have it under control." He pulled out a well-worn SAT practice book and left after giving me a big bear hug.

Johnny was an average student. Eventually he achieved an SAT score of 700. Although he didn't make it to Syracuse, he was admitted to West Connecticut State College. He'll find his success in other arenas aided by a wonderful personality and a responsive and upbeat attitude.

Dr. Ragland was always there for him, a willing friend who shared his wisdom and time and made him part of his family. Most of all, he was a true role model, embodying high standards of achievement, education, and character, the best of African American manhood.

Johnny's father did not regard the mentor as an interloper who might come between him and his son. Both men were sensitive enough and intelligent enough to understand, support, and appreciate each other's important role.

In other cases, Tyre's commandment "Thou shalt not play mother or father" was prescient. Many mentors had to be reminded that no matter how they might yearn for the parental role, they could not be mother or father. Some were childless and in some instances eager to show their affection by giving material gifts to children whose parents could not afford such expenditures. The program discouraged this behavior, but it was difficult to control.

Kareema's experience as a Riser was less successful than Johnny's. A graduate of Kenderton, she was paired with Shirley Tyree, a former middle-school counselor with a long record of caring involvement in the community, especially with children.

As this attractive 12-year-old came out of elementary school, she seemed reasonably promising, with average test scores, a fairly good academic record, fair attendance, and a good attitude towards school. She was surrounded by family members—a mother, a father, a grandmother, and at least two siblings. After making initial contacts over the phone with her mentee, Shirley arranged to pick up Kareema and her mother and drive them to the first joint meeting of Risers, parents, and mentors, to be held in one of Temple University's facilities on a spring day in 1989.

Shirley describes the occasion in detail:

"I got out of my car and knocked on the weather-beaten door, which had no working doorbell. I had no fear or apprehension. This was the kind of poor, rundown North Philadelphia neighborhood I have often seen, with abandoned, boarded-up houses. This was a block of three-story houses, which probably at one time, fifty years ago, had been part of a middle-class Jewish neighborhood. To-day, there was a vacant lot across the street; it looked like a house had been torn down. The litter and nasty trash in that space were unbelievable. All the sidewalks and curbs up and down the block were littered with stuff which looked as though it had been there for months. I looked at the guys sitting on the steps, at the teenage boys roaming up and down the block, and couldn't help thinking, 'Why don't they get off their lazy duffs and clean up this pigpen?' "

Then the door opened and ended Shirley's ruminations on environmental conditions. She was ushered into what was officially the living room, but at this point was serving other purposes. A brand-new kerosene stove radiated comforting heat, and a large double bed held a prominent place in the cluttered space. Seated upright in this bed, propped up with pillows at her back, was a woman with cropped gray hair who was obviously the matriarch of the house, the grandmother.

She looked older than she probably was, with arthritic hands. Her face was almost wrinkle-free but had a few lines that gave character to her countenance and revealed the long years of hard experience lived in poverty. She was the focal point of this household, which was "full of people all reporting to Grandma, who kept a pocketbook under the sheets," Shirley said. Apparently she controlled the money. She welcomed Shirley and expressed her approval of the Risers program, with which she seemed to be familiar.

Shirley gathered up Kareema and her mother, and they left for the meeting. The two women clicked right away. The mother was so grateful for the ride, and just "thrilled" that Kareema was a part of "such a great program." A number of times for the first two years Shirley brought the two to Risers meetings, which otherwise they probably would not have attended. The mother, a thin, rather frail woman, was always accessible and receptive.

The daughter seemed less responsive, although for the first couple of years Shirley and Kareema did plan activities together. They actually accomplished two trips, one to the museum and the other to Cheyney University. Shirley was ready and willing to do a lot more for her, but Kareema never really responded. At least twice, Shirley arranged for outings for Kareema, but when she arrived at the house at the appointed time, her mentee was nowhere to be found.

As could almost be predicted, Kareema became an unwed mother. Soon after the birth of her child, in 1993, she finally called her mentor. Despite the circumstances, this was a happy experience for Shirley, hearing Kareema say she "was thinking of me and wanted to return to school."

But in July 1994, I learned that Kareema had suffered repeated tragic losses in a short period of time—the death of her mother, then her father. Then a sister and a brother perished in a fire in a house heated by a kerosene stove.

And now, her grandmother had passed away. This was the grandmother who at one time told Shirley, "I pray that the Lord will allow me to live to see Kareema graduate from college, because she will be the first in the family."

Shirley never really gave up. "I'm going to try once more to contact her," she told me. "She needs me." She later called to tell me that when she stopped by Kareema's house, no one answered her knock. The man next door came out to tell her that the girl had moved out, and no one seemed to be living there anymore.

On a questionnaire answered by our mentors, Shirley's response to the following question revealed an upbeat attitude about what some might consider a sadly negative experience: "Do you feel that you have 'given back' and that you are making a difference in a young disadvantaged person's life?"

And her answer was, "I feel I tried, but failed. However, Kareema's memory of her mentor will be a positive image of someone who attempted to help her find the best in herself, and the best in life."

Wherever Kareema is, I hope she has clung to some of the life lessons Shirley taught her by example. Wherever she is, and whatever her condition, I hope she knows Shirley still has a warm feeling for her and fondly remembers their time together.

The mentoring experience was rich and varied. Dr. Leonard Finkelstein, a retired school superintendent, mentored Lucious Johnson. He described his experience in the Spring 1994 issue of the Risers newsletter:

> I was matched with my Riser through a drawing. It was obvious that the pairing was preordained. His first initial

is the same as that of my four children, a clear sign that we were meant for each other! I became "Uncle Len" very quickly and naturally. I gained more than a Riser. I found my life enriched by having an extended family. Lucious's mother is an incredible parent! She demanded perfect school attendance, valued and monitored his education, tried to instill the need for respect, and struggled greatly to provide for him.

Lucious is beginning his senior year. We've engaged in many activities over the last six years. He visited regularly with my family. We went fishing, took trips to farms and playgrounds, the Franklin Institute, an art show at St. Joseph's University. I looked forward to these outings and I believe he did too. But something was not working. Lucious rarely called. I asked him to keep a journal of our activities and he never seemed to do so. He did, however, write a beautiful note to Dr. Hayre mentioning some of our experiences and thanking her for the program. He was recognized as an outstanding Riser and I was proud of him. Yet, I still had a nagging concern about his lack of initiative in contacting me.

I assume every mentor-Riser relationship goes through some troubled times. It's too easy to say it didn't work out and move on. We have to ask ourselves and each other where we might have gone astray. I intend to call Lucious, read him this message, and ask him to write his version of our adventure. If my instincts are correct, we will not only have a narrative of his perceptions, but also the reawakening of our relationship.

Joan Harris, a schoolteacher, has been an exceptionally dedicated and effective mentor. She began with one Riser, then added three more. Today they're all college freshmen. Joan says:

"In 1989 mentoring was a whole new idea for me. Today I think it's an essential component for any successful youth program. I hope I've touched the lives of Monique Darby—my special Riser—as well as Katrina, Jeannette, and Yvonne. If you want to really make a difference, you have to hang in. This has been one of the most rewarding experiences in my life, but it's not always easy.

"The mentors developed close, almost filial, relationships with each other, because of our obsessive interest in our protégés. They called early in the morning and late at night to tell me Monique was elected to the Honor Society, or that Jeannette had been selected as the Spanish scholar and would be an exchange student in Spain, or that Teneshia had been asked to the senior prom."

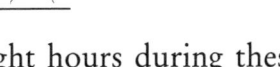

I, too, spent many late night hours during these past six years commiserating with mentors over some disappointment or unexpected difficulty. Many of these dedicated guides forgot that they had only one child to follow, while I had eighty. They were ready to talk for hours. Although our conversations were time-consuming and often emotionally exhausting, I was always willing to listen. I heard from Alma when she'd just learned her Riser was eight months pregnant. Phyllis Henderson called to tell me she was giving up on Lashonda, who seemed to have become a permanent truant.

Charles called to discuss Brian, who had dropped out of school, became involved in the drug world, and was incarcerated. Brian wanted to know if his sister, whom he described as "a really good kid," could take advantage of the Riser scholarship in his place. Brian said there was no chance of his returning to school, even though he was on

Mentors

probation, because there were people waiting to "get" him if they caught him in school. The Riser tuition money is not transferable, but we tried to solicit other aid for Brian's sister.

Linda, a senior citizen, was extremely conscientious about her mentor duties. She wanted to discuss how she could get her Riser, Cathy, back in school so that she could graduate on time. Finding child care for Cathy's infant and convincing the high school bureaucracy to make some concessions took many long hours. The fact that Cathy was pretty and bright helped. Good news: Cathy's problems were resolved. She graduated on time and enrolled at Temple in the fall of '94.

Most of our original mentors are still with the program, even those who have "lost" their charges. "Lost" in this context means students who dropped out or rejected their mentors. These mentors have continued to support the Riser program, financially or in other ways.

I am amazed at how much commitment they've given—how they've stuck through the frustrations, the disappointments, the rebuffs, to be there for youngsters so much in need of their help. But dedication was not always enough. By the beginning of their senior year, twenty-six of the Risers had dropped out despite heroic efforts on the part of their mentors.

Nevertheless, the mentors continued to be upbeat about the program. Three years after the program began, Richard Tyre conducted an informal survey of twenty-five mentors. Eighteen out of twenty-five mentors were satisfied and pleased that they had accomplished something positive. Of these, four said the Riser experience was one of the most satisfying in their lives. Five were disappointed but hoped things would improve. Two felt they had been total failures. Many mentors were pleased with the enthusiastic parental cooperation they received. As one mentor put it, "I'm using the best part of me for the next African American generation."

Chapter 10

The Pregnancy Problem

"DR. HAYRE, I HAVE BAD NEWS." I waited for Deloris James's announcement with foreboding. "Chris is pregnant and her baby is due next month." My heart sank. I knew this was bound to happen. With fifty-six girls in the Risers, it seemed unlikely that we would go six years without an occasional announcement like this.

Chris was a special-ed student, with perhaps the lowest academic potential in the class. The efforts of a wonderful mentor who had deliberately chosen to work with her couldn't prevent Chris from having two more babies and an abortion. There seemed no way to keep this large, well-developed child away from men who probably were using, even abusing, her.

The issue of teen pregnancy had reached priority proportions. In his 1995 State of the Union message, President Clinton called it "our most serious social problem." It seemed an ironic acknowledgment from the man who, two months earlier, had fired his surgeon general. Dr. Joycelyn Elders's candor and practical intelligence might have made a real difference in addressing issues of teenage sexuality. But she was too voluble and forthright, in a climate that celebrates silence.

I've often noticed that presidents, media, teachers, and preachers talk freely about violence, crime, and drugs but shy away from even a tepid discussion of problems connected with sexual relations. This squeamishness borders on a prudery reminiscent of the Victorian Age.

What impelled young girls to enter into relationships that could immeasurably damage their future? Experts advised us that Riser girls would find it difficult to deal with adolescent peer and hormonal pressures. But, I countered, what about the possibility of a better life that higher education offered?

College was only one of several options open to these young women. They might choose a two-year program with a major in a trade or life skill such as catering, cosmetology, electronics, designing, computer technology, or other occupational field. They could achieve their dreams.

It seemed imperative that we formulate plans to fight what would probably be an uphill battle. We emphasized caution in sexual relationships and discussed the dangers promiscuity presented. For backup we depended on the board-sanctioned curriculum, which emphasized abstinence. I later found out that the curriculum was not being taught—lack of resources, whatever that means, was the reason given. Programs such as "Pregnancy Is Not for Me" were carried in a few schools and seemed to have had a favorable impact on the rate of teen pregnancy. When funding dried up, those programs were terminated and the rate began to climb again.

We set up a number of information workshops involving parents, mentors, and counselors. Rashidah Hassan, the founder of BEBASHI, an organization that promotes AIDS education in the black community, presented a vibrant and interesting program. Planned Parenthood joined these efforts, working with cluster groups to emphasize the importance of sexual abstinence. Or when that seemed unrealistic, they presented the necessary admonitions concerning pregnancy, AIDS, and other sexually transmitted diseases. Regardless of these efforts, the numbers of pregnant Riser teens began to duplicate the statistics in the larger society. Pregnancies began to escalate at an alarming rate.

Twenty-two of our fifty-six girls—two in the seventh grade, four in the eighth, five in the ninth, four in the tenth, four in the eleventh, three in the twelfth—became pregnant. I would like to be able to say that this was the end, but in the first year of college, three of our girls became pregnant, although none left college.

The most heartening aspect of this sorry situation was that pregnancy did not lead to school dropouts. No girl was dismissed from the Risers program because she became pregnant. The added responsibility of single parenting made it even more important that they continue in the program. Most high schools' day-care facilities were completely filled. Some students were able to enlist the assistance of aunts, grandmothers, sisters, or their babies' fathers, but others had real problems finding caretakers.

I wallowed in frustration and disappointment as I learned of each new pregnancy. The young mothers took their new condition in stride. The federal government provided financial assistance for those who stayed in school—stipends for clothing, food, child care, and transportation.

Most of the twenty-two Riser mothers continued in the Risers program, some without missing a beat.

One Riser had her first child at sixteen and, less than a year later, a second child. She managed to earn all her high school credits by attending a private school that offered accelerated courses. It was an expensive proposition, and I don't know how she got the money. She grew up in a dysfunctional family; her mother is mentally ill and frequently hospitalized. The young woman is now in her second year of a two-year medical technology program. The children's father takes care of the babies while T., as I will call her, goes to school. She is ambitious and looks forward to receiving an associate's degree and joining the workforce.

I have tried to figure out what impels a girl to become an unwed mother. It is such an untenable situation. Still, I doubt that girls go into a relationship with pregnancy as the goal. The reasons are pretty obvious: peer pressure, a desire to be loved, and—I think this is a real need—a biologically driven curiosity that overcomes the fear of consequences. The feeling that "it can't happen to me" applies not only to pregnancy but to AIDS. I thought at its onset that AIDS would diminish sexual activity. But it seems the more we talk about it, the more people seem to be dying from the dread disease.

Today's notion that unwed parenthood is quite acceptable seems to me damaging. Yet I know that this attitude will not change by denying welfare benefits to teenage mothers. To eliminate welfare benefits would be socially irresponsible and a disaster. We cannot allow a generation of children to grow up uncared for and without the necessities of daily living.

Deloris James and I have had many conversations about this. She is one of seven children from a close-knit family with a very strong mother and father and a strong religious orientation. Deloris married at a young age, soon after high school graduation, and had seven children of her own, all of whom are now grown and successful citizens.

She believes that neither the presence nor absence of welfare money would affect the incidence of unwed teen mothers. She cites one of our Risers as an example. Kimberly comes from a home where she has been pampered by her mother and stepfather. Her grandparents dote on her in much the same measure. When Mrs. James asked Kimberly why she had gotten into this trouble—we always think of it as trouble—she said, "Mrs. James, I don't really know how I got into this situation. He kept saying how much he loved me and I began to believe him."

"Did you love him?" Mrs. James asked.

"Not really. I just got caught up in the moment, and got crazy. Anyway, I've learned my lesson." She acknowledged that the boyfriend quickly deserted her upon learning of her condition.

Certainly these are not new problems. Yet sometimes I feel inadequate in the 1990s. I seem to be from outer space. Certainly, there were instances of out-of-wedlock pregnancy when I was young. But one rarely knew about it. When there was a slip-up, a supportive family would usually ship the young woman to a relative in another city, where she would stay until the child was born and placed for adoption or cautiously brought into the family under some kind of subterfuge. The reputation of the teenager was protected.

It was rare to hear more than an occasional rumor about a pregnant student in any of the segregated high schools I taught in during the '30s. It wasn't until the '50s that I began to see premarital relationships and their consequences in out-of-wedlock pregnancies receiving increased attention, apparently a reflection of an increase in television viewing and the explosion of sex images in the media.

As principal of an all-girls school in the late fifties and early sixties I delivered regular sermonettes on the dangers of premarital sex and pregnancy. "Just tell him, 'I might think about it, but if my father ever heard about it, he would kill me.' The boy will realize you're not out there by yourself and that there is someone in your home, your father, who might take definite steps if he felt you were being taken advantage of."

My students heard these words repeated at least once each term for eight semesters during their high school years. I may be deluding myself, but I believe these speeches had an impact. Certainly, we had nothing like the number of pregnancies that we have today.

How did I handle the subject of sex with my teenage daughter? Frankly, pretty much as my mother had handled it with me—that is, mostly with silence. Occasionally I would tell her what I said during assembly, hoping to give her an idea of how I felt. But I recall no close mother/daughter discussions about the specifics of gender mores. So I was surprised when she came home during her senior year and said, somewhat reproachfully, "Mom, we have the most wonderful teacher, she has taught us all kinds of things about sexual relations, things that you never even told me about."

By the time my Risers came to me in the late 1980s we had been through the sexual revolution. Today adult cohabitation without benefit of City Hall or clergy is considered more or less routine. Adults are sophisticated about contraceptives, and it's interesting that their battle cry hinges on issues of fertility. The rate of adult out-of-wedlock births in no way equals that of the uneducated, naive teenager. In 1993 Marian Wright Edelman wrote, "The rise of adolescent pregnancy in the black community is symptomatic of the loss of hope, lack of opportunity, and poor education that is all too familiar to many black youths." I agree.

"Sex education" and "safe sex" media campaigns seem to be having little effect on teen pregnancies. Parents rarely talk about sex at home. Despite this quasi-pious silence, our society tolerates and even encourages the media onslaught of vivid and explicit sex evident on television and in X- and R-rated videos. Actually, very little can be done to curb teenage pregnancy without an overhaul of a sex-obsessed society.

What reasons did my female Risers give for going into a relationship that might end in pregnancy or HIV/AIDS? One answer was: "Well, Dr. Hayre, I was out of school and I didn't have anything to do. I hate school, I've always hated school. At any rate, I ran into a boy who was also a truant and we just got together to see what it was like, just sort of curious about it."

Another explained it this way: "I guess I was following my girlfriends. They seemed to be getting away with it, and they were telling me how great it all was. Anyway I just figured it just couldn't happen to me. But it *did* happen to me."

Or: "I was having a lot of trouble with my mom. She was trying to keep me away from boys and I really wanted to get away from her. So I went along with this man—he was more than just a teenage boy. I wasn't really in love with him but it seemed a way out of my mom's home. So I had a relationship and then I had the baby."

Although most of the girls get into these situations because of their "feelings"—hormones, I think—there is often a real need for love and affection. In his perceptive and insightful book *StreetSide,* Elijah Anderson of the University of Pennsylvania Department of Sociology describes this need:

> Up to the point of pregnancy the young man could be characterized as simply messing around. The fact of pregnancy brings a sudden reality to the relationship. She is pregnant, and he could be held legally responsible for the child's long-term financial support. Priorities begin to emerge in the boy's mind. He has to decide whether to claim the child as his or to shun the woman who has been the object of his affection.

In too many instances, as with Kimberly, the boy chooses the second option.

Still, I must disagree with Dr. Anderson's assertion, "The ignorance of inner-city girls about their bodies astonishes the middle-class observer. Many have only a vague notion of where babies come from, and they generally know nothing about birth control until after they have their first child—and sometimes not then." This is the 1990s and information is everywhere—certainly in the schools, where explicit information about human sexuality is provided from the first grade on through high school.

And what do the thirty-four girls in the program who did not become pregnant say? Jenny says: "I think the girls who had babies and quit gave up too soon. They had the opportunity to continue, but chose not to. So did the guys who dropped out, saying they had to support their child. They made money, but they are not making it legally, so what good is it?"

Margie had this to say:

My best friend Tina and I talk about it all the time. We don't understand why those girls become mothers so young. We used to hang out with them, go to the same malls, the same parties, and we turned out different. I think it's basically because of family background. My mother died when I was eight. I was raised by my dad and my two sisters. And my dad wasn't having it, okay? We lived right down the street from Kenderton and my father picked me up every day, even though it was only three minutes away. I think teenage pregnancy has a lot to do with broken families. You learn from your parents. If your parents don't give you direction, what are you going to do?

I think some of them got pregnant as an excuse not to be successful. They were scared. It's not like they were totally ignorant. They were making good grades. But they meet a guy, and he says, "I'll support you, you don't have to go to school."

I've heard all of that, but I didn't go for it.

Margie made another interesting observation. She said she began looking at boys and acting "fresh" back in the sixth grade, but the sixth-grade boys were into basketball and football and had little interest in the advances of the 12-year-old girls. By ninth grade, however, the boys' sexual interest and activity began to surge and the situation became totally different.

This lamentation has dealt mainly with the girls. However, at least seven of the fifty-eight teenage boys became fathers, although—perhaps surprisingly—there were no relationships between Risers that led to pregnancy. The boys we know about acknowledged their parenthood and, in some instances, continue to contribute to their children's welfare.

When I meet these young parents, who are holding their babies with obvious love and affection, it's hard to believe there's not something wholesome and healthy at work here. It's impossible to resist the smiles and coos of a dear little human being, so new to this awful world. Despite the odds facing them, I say a prayer: "May God be with you, and make you a blessing for this world."

Chapter 11

Mission Accomplished

A GENTLE SUMMER BREEZE wafted through the wide stained-glass windows of Temple University's Mitten Hall. This was the Riser high school graduation, the culminating event—on June 24, 1994—that I had anticipated for six years. I actually pinched myself to be sure it was really happening. How quickly the years had passed and how full they had been. Here I was, a grand old 83, and beginning to feel the weight of those years. But I had survived!

As a matter of fact I was attending this event against doctor's orders. Twenty-four hours earlier I had been hospitalized with an irregular heartbeat. Although it had been quickly regulated, the emergency room doctor had insisted on admitting me to intensive care. I told him and each of the other four examining doctors that I would be leaving the next morning. I had a commitment I was determined to keep.

The next morning at eight I got out of the hospital bed, dressed, called for a doctor, and signed a release form. My daughter picked me up and took me home before going on to her job.

That afternoon, relieved and happy, I sat on stage, waiting for the ceremony to begin. The auditorium quickly filled with parents and friends as well as the extended Riser family of teachers, counselors, and mentors. The purr of gentle conversation, punctuated by the occasional shriek of reunited friends, filled the room. I recognized many folks I had grown to love over the past six years.

In the weeks before the ceremony we had seemed to be living in a haze of perpetual rehearsals. The thirty-nine graduates attended seventeen different high schools and had been immersed in plans for those graduation ceremonies. It had been difficult to arrange rehearsals for the commemorating Riser event. I was a bit nervous about how it would turn out.

The graduates had decided to wear the caps and gowns they had worn during the previous week's commencement exercises. The red and white class colors of Gratz, the blue of West Philadelphia, the gold and white of Olney, and the hues of fourteen other high schools made their own happy claim to the afternoon's celebration. The Risers were to march in, as they had six years earlier at Kenderton and Wright Schools. Instead of being seated on the stage behind me, they would fill the four facing rows.

Ron James, who had done such a superb mentoring job, took his seat at the piano and the room hushed as "Pomp and Circumstance" once again echoed throughout the room. All eyes were fixed on the rear of the auditorium as Elaine Abrams, who had graduated in the top fifth

The Risers in all their finery on graduation day 1994.

of her class at Martin Luther King High School, led her cohort of graduating Risers down the aisle. I realized I was crying—yes, me, the hardy, usually unemotional old soul was uncontrollably moved.

The strong final chord sent the to-be-seated signal. Another two rows of Risers were seated behind the graduates. These young men and women were a year behind their class, but were determined to graduate in the class of 1995. I was equally proud of them.

The dean of Temple's College of Education, Dr. Trevor Sewell, introduced Temple president Peter Liacouras, Mayor Ed Rendell, and other officials who extended greetings and congratulations. Riser Monique Darby welcomed them, saying, "We are here to mark the end of one era, and the beginning of another."

The Risers had unanimously chosen Dr. Constance Clayton, our distinguished former superintendent, to deliver their graduation message. Her words of inspiration were gripping: "You have had a tremendous opportunity, provided by an educator whose life is so full of accomplishments that few can match the honor and respect associated with her name. She has taught us that there is dignity and purpose to life, that success is achieved through pride in oneself, respect for one's colleagues, loyalty to a cause, and good, honest hard work." She charged the Risers to make the most of the opportunity they had been given. "Ladies and gentlemen, you are the creators of tomorrow's better ideas. . . . You will determine how ideas are put to use, and who ultimately benefits. . . . You are at a pivotal point in defining who you are and who you ought to be. Your choices are limitless."

I was proud of my kids as they received her words of inspiration—eyes bright, minds alert, obviously moved by her speech. Other words of note that afternoon came from Deloris James and others. The high point of the afternoon was the Risers' group rendition of Maya Angelou's poem "And Still I Rise." They had rehearsed it for weeks, but their delivery had been as uneven as their attendance. Edith Stephens signaled them to stand. And the words began to flow:

> You may shoot me with your words
> You may cut me with your eyes
> You may kill me with your hatefulness
> But still, like air, I'll rise
> Out of the huts of history's shame
> I rise
> Up from a past that's rooted in pain
> I rise

I'm a black ocean, leaping and wide
Welling and swelling I bear in the tide
Bringing the gifts that my ancestors gave
I am the dream and the hope of the slave
I rise
I rise
I rise!

As the last "I rise!" rang out, the audience was clearly moved. I felt a teardrop or two trickling down my shiny nose again. Amid loud applause, the Risers sat, visibly relieved that this part of the program was over.

As they crossed the stage to receive their Riser medallions and certificates of tuition assistance, each student gave me a hug. I looked out over these young people seated before me. I admired their achievements. I knew it had not been easy for many. They had persevered and won one of life's most important battles, the battle for self.

During the past six years, they had played an active role in almost every memorable occasion in my life. I remembered those Omega Christmas parties where we ate very well, played games, and danced the Electric Slide— which I knew—as well as more energetic dances that were quite foreign to me. When the Southwest Belmont YWCA honored me in 1989, it was Katy who made the touching and eloquent introduction. She was only 13 at the time and had been carefully coached by mentor Edith Stephens.

When I was inducted as president of the board of education, there they were, ten of them, so proud when they were introduced as Risers and asked to stand. Even after those first six years, many of the Risers have remained a part of my life. At an event given by the Afro-American Museum in my honor, Wendell Griffith came all the way from Lincoln University. He spoke extemporaneously and

I celebrated most of the special occasions with Risers during those six years. This was a little birthday celebration at Temple University during a Saturday morning Risers Club session.

glowingly about the Riser program. "I never even thought about some day going to college," he said, "until she came along and promised that scholarship."

When Alpha Kappa Alpha sorority had featured Wendell, Shawn, Michael, and Khalil as escorts during its grand annual Calendar Girl Gala, they were big hits, elegantly attired in tuxedos with the formal dress shirt, tie, and cummerbund. They performed impeccably, bowing, dancing, and pacing their young ladies. Khalil was chosen Mr. Personality. I watched the event feeling like some kind of proud mother—or more properly—grandmother. At the end of the program I hugged each one of these four tall, strong young men, whom I first met as 12-year-olds and who were now on their way to college.

In the next chapter, I will tell you the stories of some of the Risers—both the successes we celebrated at that graduation ceremony on June 24, 1994, and two that had a different ending. But at this moment when I recall for you that day of triumph, I want to give the last word to Risers president Wendell Griffith, whose story you will read, and whose moving words closed the ceremony: "Never give up on your dreams, because we are young, black, intelligent, and on the right track. In life, when you fall, get back up. When you trip, keep your balance. Remember to keep your head and shoulders above the rest."

Chapter 12

The Risers

Even among the many success stories of the Risers, Wendell Griffith's was unique. Wendell was the only Riser to take full opportunity of the desegregation opportunity, attending predominantly white middle and senior high schools. He tells his story eloquently:

"I went to Kenderton, LaBrum Middle School in northeast Philadelphia, and George Washington High School in the far northeast. My mom really didn't want me to go to Gillespie, the neighborhood middle school. Back then, the drug scene was really bad. The drugs were hitting the neighborhood hard, and she wanted me to stay as far away from it as possible. I was the only Riser at LaBrum, but it was okay. I looked at it as a challenge. I had never gone to school with white kids before, and they pretty much all thought they were smarter than black kids. I think I handled it pretty well. I made white friends, too, and I worked really hard to prove black kids were

Wendell

smart. And then I found out I was smarter than a lot of them. It wasn't a racist school or anything like that, but it was different in that it helped me mature in a lot of ways.

"It took forty-five minutes to get there from my home. Every morning for a year my mom woke me up. Because I'm a very slow person in the mornings, I had to get up at five o'clock to have enough time to get dressed, eat breakfast, make it to the bus stop, and arrive at school by 7:15.

"I did the same thing at George Washington High. I wanted to go to Gratz with my friends, but my mom said, 'No, no, you're going to George Washington, you're doing well.' So I said, 'Well, okay.'

"I really got tired of it but I stuck it out for four years, and I'm glad. Now I'm at Lincoln University and I am really pleased. I wanted to be with my own people, and absorb all our culture and our ways. Lincoln is such an important black college, I'm happy to be there.

"My mentor is Kenneth Harper of Omega Psi Phi fraternity and Bell Telephone. He has taught me a lot of things about college in general and Lincoln specifically that I've learned are true. He took me to high school football games to see his son play. We did other things together, too. I look up to him. I wanted to come to Lincoln ever since the Risers visited the school in eighth grade. It's very peaceful and I wanted to get away from that city lifestyle.

"When the Riser program began, I thought this is great, all of us getting a chance at a college education like that. But people started making choices in their lives in the eighth and ninth grade, choosing to be drug dealers, or criminals, or dropouts, or pregnant. Some of us chose college. It's hard to believe that some people didn't make that choice. I mean, I played high school basketball and a little football, but the football started interfering with my studies. I'd get up, go to classes, go to practice. By the time I got home, I was exhausted because football wears you right out, and I didn't do my schoolwork like I should. So I quit football. I chose college.

"I've decided right now to get a degree in health and physical education, to be a counselor of some sort. I had a lot of things to prove when I got here at Lincoln. For some reason I thought I wasn't going to make it. But I'm determined. And I owe a lot of people; I owe my parents, and the Risers program. My grades at Lincoln were good the first term; I have a 3.2 average. I have a summer job lined up at a day-care center. I'm looking forward to that. Once I get my degree I can help a lot of other, older kids."

Khalil was a youngster who had plenty to overcome—no functioning parent, poverty, and an environment rife with ills and temptations. Khalil says:

"Being in the Risers taught me that things that look impossible can really happen. I was a typical Joe off the street, and I had other things against me. I was born addicted to heroin, my mother and father abandoned me. My grandmother took care of me since I was thirteen months old. I was always a problem child. If I didn't like something, I didn't do it. I was left back in the fifth grade, and in the seventh grade. I didn't care about school. But when I got to Strawberry Mansion Middle School and received the tutoring and support the Riser program provided, I began to get A's and B's. When I saw that I could do the work, I knew I could go to college. I was upgraded as my work improved but I still didn't have enough credits to graduate, so I went on to summer school. And then I was accepted at Morehouse. Now I'm in college. College. The Risers program has had a major effect on my life. When I begin my professional life I plan to credit the Risers Club for a major, major part of my success.

"I became the father of a young lad thirteen months ago. I plan to do well by my child. That's one thing wrong with black men; they don't have enough fathers. When I'm home on break I spend a great deal of time with my son. My family takes care of him while I'm at school, and I'm very comfortable with that. I have to do my job at Morehouse. These four years will be better for him in the long run."

Much credit for Khalil's success must be given to the Strawberry Mansion Middle–Senior High School com-

Khalil

plex. They may well be the best secondary school in North Philadelphia. The most noteworthy aspect of this relatively small school is its leadership, especially its two most recent principals, Karen DelGuercio and Clyde Basham. They brought remarkable dedication, talent, compassion, and concern to their jobs.

Mansion, as it's fondly called, was also blessed with outstanding, hardworking college counselors who went far beyond the call of duty to help students. There were seven Riser students at Mansion, none originally considered superior students. But the seven Risers stayed the course and all were accepted into college except two special-ed pupils who were mainstreamed into special occupational training.

I'm somewhat reluctant to write about Katy because she really tried to keep her very serious problems from peers as well as teachers. Her mentor is well aware of her terrific struggles. Katy, the oldest of five children, was born to a mother with severe drug problems. She had left the children in the care of their grandmother.

Because of repeated absences, Katy began to fail many subjects in high school. She was capable of much more than she was producing. I remembered an impressive speech she delivered at a luncheon sponsored by the YWCA. Actually she was introducing me as one of the honorees. I was surprised when I learned that the girl who had made such a brilliant showing had become a chronic absentee and was failing most of her work.

I discovered that Katy was the glue that held her siblings together. Their home was cramped and rather bedraggled—the five children had to share one bedroom. Katy made sure her little sisters got off to school each morning, properly dressed and with their hair freshly braided. Then she would get herself together and go to school—late, of course.

Despite these burdens, Katy was able to turn her luck around. When her mother overcame her addiction and remarried, Katy was able to give up some of the responsibility for the younger children. She returned to school and, by taking extra courses, made up most of her failures. Katy is an example of a young woman who has beaten the odds through sheer determination, and emerged a winner.

"My second period report card is good," she says. "I'm going to the 20th Century Math program at Temple five days a week. I want to go to college and make something out of my life. I want to take up nursing, or become a paralegal.

"The Riser program taught me to never say never. If you want to accomplish something, you have to push to accomplish it. If ever I get any money, I'd really like to do for other young people what Dr. Hayre has done for us."

Shawn was classified as learning disabled when he left Wright School. If Shawn was ever lacking in math or language skills, he's certainly made up for it in motivation, character, and determination. After Wright, he went on to FitzSimons Middle School, where he was mainstreamed—placed in regular classes with students who were unlabeled. He performed quite well in most of the academic subjects.

Shawn says, "I'm waiting for an apprenticeship in a mortuary business before I go to college. You have to have an apprenticeship first. Mrs. James has been working with me.

"I remember when Dr. Hayre made the Riser announcement. Actually my grandmother had to explain it to me. My grandmother pointed out that people don't often give black kids that kind of chance. So I was thankful from the start. I had rarely thought about college before that. My grandmother kept encouraging me and explaining what was needed.

"At first I really wasn't too sure about this program. I didn't want to go to the meetings because they were on Saturdays. I was about to skip the meeting when Dr. Hayre called one morning and said, 'Get yourself up and come down here. You all are my grandkids and I'm counting on you.' So I went down to Bright Hope Baptist Church. I was really shocked that she called me personally.

Shawn

"The tutoring sessions helped a lot, especially the college prep material. I liked the trips, especially the visit to Fellowship Farm.

"Even though I'm young, I've been to a lot of funerals in my lifetime. The first one was my great-grandmother's. Then my uncle, my dad, and my aunt died. I went to one friend's funeral in November and another in January.

"I always found mortuary work interesting. One time the program took the Risers to the morgue and that was great—to see everything they use and so forth. It's a solid business and you can't fail because people die every day.

"I went to Strawberry Mansion Middle and High School and it was fine. The principal, Mr. Basham, and the vice principal, Mr. Kenny, were both very hard on us Risers. They'd keep saying, 'You know you have a college scholarship waiting for you, so don't mess up. Do your work, go to class, don't let me see you wandering.' My grandmother made sure I was on time to school and all that.

"I didn't go the fast money way, because I knew I'd be dead or in jail. My grandmother made sure I didn't, and, like I said, I didn't want to anyway.

"One of my mentors, Miss Edith Stephens, got me into the AKA Calendar Girl pageant. I was one of the escorts. I really liked learning the proper way to do things like bow and how to walk.

"The main thing I learned from the Risers program is that you have to be independent and work for what you get because it's not going to come easy for black kids. You have to work hard. You have to count on yourself."

Shawn, who is already a success, is a fine example of a young black man's aspirations and determination.

We lost twenty-six out of the 116 original Risers along the way. Some just vanished from their neighborhoods. Four students disappeared before the sixth-grade graduation from elementary school. They were not in school and never even heard my promise. Attendance officers tried to track them down, but two were never found and the other two surfaced as teenage mothers. Some were dropped or pushed out before Deloris James was notified. Before we even began, the number had shrunk to 112.

Deloris James, mentors, teachers, and I all tried to reclaim the twenty-six dropouts. Our efforts were, for the most part, futile. The promise of "Tell Them We Are Rising" was not enough to save them or make them realize the value of staying in school and out of trouble. The dubious rewards of the drug trade seduced at least four Risers.

Perhaps it was too much to hope that all 112 students could escape the grip of a culture that ranks instant gratification above delayed rewards, sensual pleasures over intellectual pursuits, tantalizing material trinkets over intangible internal satisfactions.

Ray's case is the most egregious example of how poorly the schools handle children with multiple social problems; how adult prejudices can doom a child's academic and social chances almost from the beginning; and how—despite valiant efforts from concerned adults—such children are often banished from society.

Ray entered the Risers program with several strikes against him, a not uncommon condition among poor black children. By the time he entered sixth grade he had been suspended several times. Although he read on grade level and could do math adequately, Ray had developed a dislike for school. Conditions at home were playing havoc with any possible emotional and educational success. Ray told his mentor, who was experienced in counseling disabled children, that his father, who had been in prison since Ray was four, was scheduled to be released on probation. Ray hated his father and hoped he would never see him again. Ray's grandmother had gained legal custody of the boy and his brothers. She was, and is, the only stable force in his life, displaying constant devotion, care, help, and support.

Ray's family was poor, having little more than the necessities, and he worked after school and on weekends earning money for basic goods. He gradually developed a good relationship with his mentor but continued to have trouble with school.

"School stinks. I'm always blamed for things I didn't do" was his refrain. His record showed constant suspensions and failing grades. Clearly, he was heading for disaster.

Hoping to avert what seemed inevitable, his grandmother and mentor regularly visited his middle school. The first visit set the tone, one of disparagement, prejudice, and do-nothingness. His mentor describes that fateful visit this way:

"When I introduced myself as Ray's mentor, the counselor, teachers, and assistant principal came running to complain about Ray. I stopped them all in their tracks when I asked them to tell me one good thing about Ray. They did not respond and continued with their complaints.

"When I asked what we could do to help Ray, everyone laughed. Just get him out of our class, they said. The assistant principal said even corporal punishment was not effective. Ray was disliked by all the adults he met with at school. How could he succeed in this environment?"

Sadly, the answer turned out to be that Ray could not. Meetings with school staff became more frequent but less effective. No one implemented any of the suggestions or strategies his mentor, who was an educator, offered. They continued to blame the child, without examining their own flaws.

Before long, Ray was accused of slashing a teacher's tires and was transferred to another school. Instead of a clean slate and a fresh start, his reputation preceded him. Nothing changed. He was frequently suspended, and got zeroes on tests he missed while on suspension. Through all this, his grandmother and his mentor made constant visits to the school. Ray eventually had to go to summer school to pass into the eighth grade. The surprising thing is that he actually did go, and he made up his failures.

By now his father had been released from prison, but his homecoming only worsened the situation. Ray began appearing in school with bruises administered by his father during bouts of drunkenness. Apparently no teacher, no counselor, no one at the school noticed the bruises or the fingermarks on his face. Ray reported the situation to the school, but again, nothing was done. One beating was so severe Ray had to call the police. Finally Ray ran away, going ten miles to his mentor's home. Ray made it clear he would never go home again. His grandmother struck a deal with the mentor to keep Ray until things calmed down.

During the week he stayed with his mentor, Ray calmed down in school. No complaints came from the school about his behavior. But when he returned home, still against his wishes, it was not long before his school behavior was again a problem.

Finally his grandmother took him to a mental health clinic for psychiatric help. After months of weekly visits, Ray was discharged with a clean bill of health. Unfortunately his family and school problems continued. So Ray turned for comfort to new, older "friends"—teenagers who already were in trouble with the law. They began to have more and more influence on his thoughts and actions, despite attempts by his grandmother, his mentor, Deloris James, and even me to keep him on target. Ray was teetering on the edge of dropping out.

Finally an opportunity came for Ray to receive positive recognition. The school sponsored a fashion show for which backdrops were needed. Ray, a talented artist, was asked to paint some of the scenery. Although everyone was pleased with Ray's work, his name was omitted from the program and he got no accolades or recognition at the fashion show. I found it difficult to understand, much less condone, such flagrant insensitivity on the part of adults.

Ray managed to graduate from middle school—not an easy task. Throughout the summer, he worked during the day and became more involved with his "friends" at night. He got deeper and deeper into the code of the streets. Incidents piled up in which Ray had played a role, and finally he entered the court system and was sentenced to Glen Mills, a youth detention center located in a rural area about twenty miles from Philadelphia.

Fourteen months later he was released with a record of good behavior, but it wasn't long before Ray was in front of a judge again. This time he was ordered into Vision Quest, a program for troubled youth. When he returned home, his grandmother is reported to have shipped him off to New York to other relatives. No one, including his mentor, has heard from Ray in over a year. His family has dispersed. He is truly gone with the winds of poverty and institutional neglect. Ray was my closest brush with what we term "juvenile delinquent." Yet whenever I met him at the social events his mentor insisted he attend, I was impressed with his attractive, almost cherubic face and mild, friendly demeanor.

The school system's indifference to Ray's case was duplicated in lesser degrees with other Risers, particularly boys. I personally intervened in some cases where I knew teachers had let either prejudice or laziness guide their responses to these children.

The fact that African American boys suffer the highest rates of punishments and suspensions must be addressed, and accountability for this national condition assigned. I have to think that the lingering, unspoken bias and fear of black men is at the root of many of these actions. This officially sanctioned behavior and the attendant absence of teacher/parental accountability engender the anger and indifference that many black male students feel.

Patricia, a pretty little girl who showed great academic promise, first attracted my attention during elementary school commencement exercises. At her mother's insistence Patricia went to a Catholic middle school, where she made excellent grades. For ninth grade she was accepted at Girls High, the city's prestigious academic high school, but she lasted only one year before flunking all of her subjects. So she returned to Gratz, her neighborhood high school, and again began capturing A's and B's on her report cards. Apparently the Girls High experience had done little to damage her self-esteem.

Patricia was exemplary in her adjustment to the Risers program. During her year at Girls High she regularly attended the Saturday sessions. She was elected president of the Risers Club and was diligent in trying to motivate others to attend. She enrolled in summer school to make up the subjects she had failed at Girls High. She did so well during her remaining high school years that she was elected to the National Honor Society in her senior year and was accepted into Bloomfield State College, with full financial aid, including a substantial Riser grant.

She was one of our successes and absolutely the last Riser I expected to go astray. Were there any clues in her behavior and attire at Risers meetings that could have warned us to keep a closer eye on her? I think not.

Patricia became friendly with another Riser named Dora, who had done well in elementary school but began to fail subjects in middle school and entered high school a year behind her class. The two girls were attractive, slim, blooming with youthful energy and free from the usual adolescent curses of acne and baby fat. They began to appear at Riser activities in lavish makeup, with elaborate, overdone hairdos, garbed in the softest-quality leathers and expensive top-of-the-line sneakers. I took note of their getups—as anyone who was not blind would have—but dismissed their behavior as a more blatant example of the premium all teenagers place on dress and appearance.

My first inkling that all was not well came when a Riser boy, a close neighbor and friend of Patricia's, confided to his mentor that he had seen the two girls dancing nude in one of the sleaziest dives in North Philadelphia. He had confronted Patricia, who laughed and dismissed his admonitions as weak and irrelevant. "I get paid $100, $200, $300 a night. I can do anything I want, I don't have anything to be ashamed of," she bragged. "I'm getting paid, that's all. Why do you care?"

His mentor called another mentor, and the two decided to tell me. I was shocked and asked Deloris James to look into it. I mentioned the incident to an associate superintendent of schools but he didn't seem as disturbed about it as I. Deloris and I both discussed the situation with a nonteaching assistant at Gratz who said he would find out if Patricia was dancing there and if so what action might be taken. He later described the club, a long, narrow room with a scratched wooden bar and an elevated circular platform that served as a stage, backlit with red and white bulbs, silvery spangled curtains, and several metal poles striped like a barber's symbolic totem. Patrons could buy a private dance, and the dancer herself, at highly inflated prices. It was a raw marketplace of sensation, truly "ugly as sin."

After hearing the assistant's report, Deloris confronted Patricia, who denied the story and swore that she never had danced in the place and that she never would.

Patricia was scheduled to graduate in June and insisted that she wanted to attend college. But her extracurricular activities had become known to other Risers. If I ignored the matter, what lesson would the Risers learn? If I tried to treat it as just another unfortunate detour, like an unplanned baby, what message would that send? Since nude dancing by underage girls was clearly illegal, how could I hold my head up if I didn't try to intervene?

I called Patricia at home and left an urgent message. She was to meet me at Gratz immediately after school. She was wide-eyed with wonder that anyone, much less dear Dr. Hayre, could believe she would stoop to such behavior. No, she swore, she never did such a thing and couldn't do such a thing.

I listened as expressionlessly as possible and then said, "Patricia, whatever may have happened before now, I cannot do anything about. If you don't value yourself enough to keep from behaving this way, I don't suppose I can do anything about that either. But I can and will do something about the future. If you continue this activity you will no longer be part of the Risers. This is my final word. I cannot condone illegal activity by any of my Risers and I will not reward you by providing your tuition."

Patricia's eyes began to tear, her voice quavered as she again protested her innocence, and then, in a contradiction only a teenager could devise, promised never to do it again. This vow may have lasted a week or two. But after graduation, we learned that Patricia was dancing again on the same stage, this time with a couple of close friends.

I was heartsick. But Patricia was now 18, and there was nothing we could legally do. She had graduated from high school, filled out the college admission forms, and was duly accepted at one of the state universities, with all of her tuition and most of her room and board covered.

Patricia never made it to college. Earlier this year, two Riser boys said they had seen her in the wee hours of the morning, getting rides and money from some popular Philadelphia rappers and bragging about her trip to Puerto Rico with one rapper, wearing the gold jewelry she received as a gift from another.

The fact that rap star Easy E was dying of AIDS as a result of the same lifestyle that Patricia had adopted didn't make a dent in Patricia's new shell of greed, they said. Her mother encourages her to take all she can get from the men. Her brother loathes Patricia's activities but has no influence with her at all. To lose this young woman was both infuriating and heartbreaking. But she made a choice, one that could cost her her life.

As I write these vignettes of Riser students I ponder what it is that makes for success or failure. Can success be predicted? Can failure be foreseen? At what age?

I brought out the list of Kenderton sixth-graders I had been given six years earlier with the pertinent information about each student, that is, standardized test scores, economic status, and family composition. Before I knew anything about these students, I concluded that of the forty-eight in the class, twenty-nine gave every indication of academic success. This translates to 60 percent, just about the graduation rate for the average comprehensive high school.

I was not far wrong in my prediction. Those who showed signs of success at sixth grade ultimately did succeed. There were a few miscalculations, however, which simply prove that in this life, one cannot count on anything for sure. Susan and Tamla, who seemed so promising, were among the casualties, although they have as much, even more, going for them than many other students in the class.

Of the sixty-four Wright School graduates, thirty-seven were "regulars" and twenty-seven were special-education students. Twenty-one of the "regular" students and six special-ed students, labeled learning disabled—twenty-seven in all—earned high school diplomas.

What seem to be the key indicators for school success?

The support and guidance of some significant adult. In every case of success, the student had at least one strong parent, usually the mother but sometimes the father, and occasionally an intact family, mom and dad both. Sometimes the grandmother was the anchor. Some successful students credit their achievements to the influence of an effective and caring mentor.

Academic ability and interest in learning. The pupils who enter school in first grade and almost immediately have difficulty learning will quickly fall by the wayside unless given much special help and attention. This is often available for students who are put in special-education categories and may account for the fact that five of the twelve students who were labeled learning disabled were able to "move" and succeed in mainstream classes.

Moral fiber, the will to succeed, the student's ambition, determination, energy, and motivation. Why a boy on one side of the street with all the factors in his favor succeeds, and a classmate with almost identical factors who lives across the street fails, remains puzzling. Boy number one is a success, a blessing to his parents and his teachers, and an asset to his school; boy number two winds up failing his parents, his teachers, and his community, sometimes even ending up in delinquent or criminal activities. Can we explain why boy number one takes one path, and boy number two takes the destructive road? I guess the old hymn may apply: "Something within me / I cannot explain."

I write these words almost eight years since I first laid eyes on those 12-year-old children. I could have insulated my life from the realities of their lives. But I'm so glad I followed my heart and took this leap of faith. I would have missed so much that expanded the dimensions of my being, that helped me discover reservoirs of patience and tolerance, of hope and faith, of understanding and compassion. Being involved with these young people added years to my life and life to my years, and I shall be forever grateful.

Chapter 13

What I Have Learned

W HEN THE WORDS "Tell Them We Are Rising" were first spoken over 130 years ago, I'm sure they ended with an exclamation mark. For Richard Robert Wright and the thousands of his contemporaries so recently released from the humiliating and degrading condition of slavery, there was no way to go but up. And up they went, through the white hatred and vitriolic meanness of the South, the lynch mobs, the Klan, the sharecropping farms where conditions were just a mini-step removed from slavery. This race of incredibly hard workers persevered through back-breaking labor, menial and poorly paid jobs, and unremitting assaults on body and spirit. And in one generation—less than a hundred years—their children had become physicians, dentists, and entrepreneurs with a presence in every Southern town and city.

They were owners and operators of barbershops, hotels, insurance companies, newspapers, dance halls, grocery stores, and beauty parlors. They became educators who tended to the education crucial to masses of unlettered ex-slaves. Many became preachers and established, usually with the nickels and dimes of the congregation, churches that became the heart and seat of African American influence and power. They taught in black schools and colleges—Wilberforce in Ohio, Atlanta University in Georgia, Cheyney (originally the Institute for Colored Youth) and Lincoln in Pennsylvania. Most of these institutions were started as a result of white philanthropy. But others were founded by church denominations, black and white.

With this history and today's opportunities, the 1990s should be a wonderful time for my Risers. Yet almost one-half of them were unable to live up to the opportunity. Some of my well-intentioned pedagogical friends let me know they felt I would be wasting my money on a group of children who, they thought, showed little promise of academic success.

Watering down curriculum, having low expectations, and generally discounting students from poor neighborhoods are some of the biggest criticisms leveled at teachers. They look at the statistics—the number of dropouts, truants, teen mothers, incarcerated; listen to the gloom-and-doom conversations of colleagues; and ponder the profile and record of their charges.

I was a savvy educator. I knew what the odds were and I chose to keep the faith.

The contradictions between my strict, sheltered upbringing and my Risers' often free-form, unrestricted development, the contrast between my acceptance of delayed gratification for later reward and their urgent pursuit of immediate pleasures, all intrigue and frustrate me.

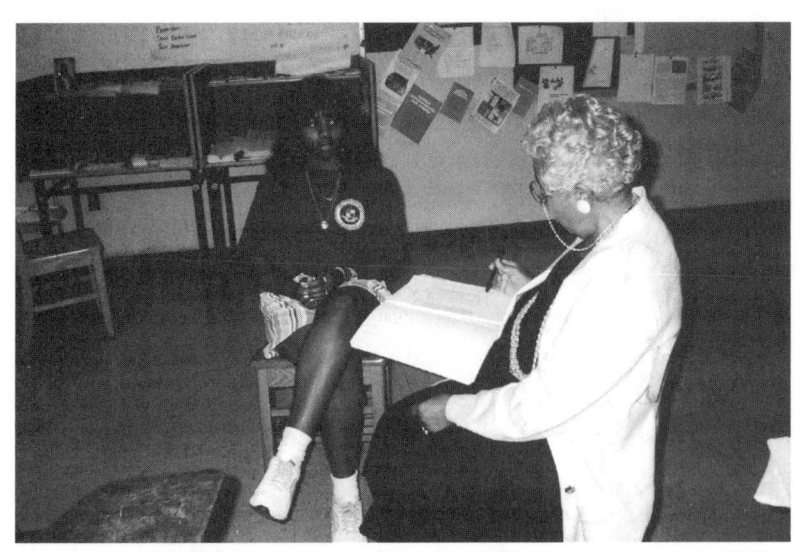

Here I am with Riser Tracey Stanton going over her grades at Germantown High.

But contrary to the expectations of some elitists and cynics, these contrasts never interfered with the mutual affection, and in some cases love, that developed between us. The Risers' emotional needs were often cloaked by indifference and hostility towards adults who tried to supply the guidance and discipline they secretly craved. But I think we fulfilled those needs for many.

Too often I was flabbergasted by the many changes the children had to cope with, changes they had little control over—the early onset of physical maturity, parents dying or disappearing into prison or addiction, the shift from easy academic success in elementary school to abysmal failures in middle and high school and the change from eagerness to confront obstacles to apathetic lethargy at the sheer numbers of those barriers.

I did my best to keep private my appalled reactions to these difficulties, and I was thankful to have been spared such agonies so early in my life. And yet these many challenges, including the public's disregard for their young lives, has not daunted them, or me. In that, we have a bond that cannot be broken.

So often I have wished I could turn back the clock for them so they could grow up protected by the comfort of a committed family, spiritual guidance through regular church attendance, a circle of watchful, loving friends and neighbors. Yet at other times I envied their freely given opinions and theories about life—unheard of from children in my day—their independent, intellectual searches for meaning in life, even if they sometimes went off half-cocked or comically astray.

I have lived with all the plagues of the modern world. I have battled racism, sexism, poverty, and neglect and have won a fair number of fights. Perhaps my longevity and continued good health account for my optimism and confidence. I am convinced that schools will become smaller, better places designed to help children realize their best potential. And I believe some of my Risers will help make this happen.

The lessons I learned from my Risers are numerous and varied. This chapter will explore several of them:

• **Conditions in the 1990s are increasingly worse for children than they have been since the child-labor era.** This is true not only for poor children, but for all children. America has never been utopia for its kids. Today's culture is hostile to children, swallowing up, immersing and destroying so many of them. Our children are victimized by violence and by the ever-prevalent obsession with sex and its larger consequences, pregnancy, abortions, and AIDS. They are traumatized and psychologically damaged by living without limits imposed by loving parents. Only the strong survive and, on the positive side, there are many who are strong.

• **Schools in predominantly poor neighborhoods often do not work for large numbers of children.** This becomes more evident as the child proceeds—notice I did not say "progresses"—through school. How else do we account for a 50 to 60 percent dropout rate and a daily absentee mark of 40 percent at the senior high level?

The 1990s schools are faced with more violence, more crime, more guns, more drugs, more poverty, more babies born to teenage mothers. All this during a period when resources for education, for health care, for employment seem to have almost dried up. Changing these conditions will not be easy.

• **The middle school is a mistake.** So were the junior high schools that started as a "noble experiment" well over a half century ago. The Philadelphia school system was hastily reorganized from junior highs into "middle schools" a few years ago. I'm not sure why. Certainly there has been no improvement in attendance, grades, or retention. Nationwide statistics indicate that the largest number of poor attenders and dropouts are to be found in the middle school. My Risers left the sixth grade for "middle schools" and that's where they began to fall apart—failing grades, truancy, poor attitudes towards school and teachers, and antisocial behavior. They would have fared better if they could have continued with seventh and eighth grades in their elementary schools.

This change from elementary school to a new building distant from their neighborhoods, with new teachers and a roster of diverse subjects taught in several different rooms, is unsettling for many inner-city kids with already erratic lives. The seeds of nonattendance and dropout status are planted right here. When the time comes to make the next change, to the senior high, an even larger structure with new rules, new teachers, and a new principal, it is often more than the pupil can handle.

Why not eliminate one of these rites of passage and restructure our schools to return to the kindergarten through eighth grade elementary school and the ninth through twelfth senior high school? The K–8 organization offers young people a much-needed stability and continuity. At the very least, the middle-school concept needs to be reevaluated.

• **We must find alternative methods for delivering education to at-risk youngsters.** Former superintendent Dr. Constance Clayton preferred the term "of value" to "at-risk." Every human being has value. It is distressing to see so many teenagers, especially boys, dissipating their value in such self-destructive behavior as truancy, street crime, and overall rejection of school.

Why won't they go to school? They have nothing better to do during that in-between stage—12 through 18 years of age. So why not school? Schools are safer places than street corners and vacant lots. Yet these children seem allergic to the schools they are required to attend. Occupational schools and "alternative" schools are possibilities worth exploring.

We've "lost" at least twenty-eight Risers since 1988. I believe most of them would have responded to an occupational or alternative school setting with a "magnet" flavor.

One possibility is a sports-oriented school, with math and business skills reinforced in the context of sports statistics and the income athletics generate. A music school is, of course, a natural, with an emphasis on the business skills needed to manage a music career. There are purists who would call this kind of accommodation "sugarcoating" education. Perhaps at one time, before I worked with the Risers, I would have deemed it sugarcoating, too. But today's children have taught me better.

Other alternative school settings are the all-black-male school—classes for black males only have proven successful in the lower grades—and the Afrocentric school, which focuses on world history, culture, and so on from the African, not European, perspective without excluding the latter.

Philadelphia has been in the national forefront for years in developing and setting standards for vocational and technical education. State-of-the-art skills centers have broadened this opportunity. These schools have tended to be selective, setting admissions standards based on previous academic record, attendance, and behavior.

Eight of my Risers were accepted at Dobbins Area Vocational-Technical High School. All eight graduated and were admitted to college. They took the necessary courses for college admission, but they also had a trade major such as restaurant practice, computer science— Dobbins was a pioneer in this field thirty years ago— health care, or one of many other areas. The school day consisted of eight instead of the usual five periods, and lasted an hour and a half longer.

Children who are dropouts might be reclaimed and given the skills that can help them make it through life. The regular school, as it is presently constituted, does not appear capable of doing so.

I asked one Riser, who had been sent to Boone, a disciplinary school, and had done so well that he was being transferred to a regular high school, how he liked Boone. He replied, "I liked it, and I wish I could have stayed."

"What did you like and why?" I asked.

He answered, "They had discipline, they made you behave yourself, and they learned you something."

A little more discipline and a better-crafted, more effective curriculum might help these kids "on the edge" of leaving school and losing out on a productive life.

 • **Too many kids are floundering because they need a one-to-one relationship with a concerned adult.** Many adolescents are alienated from the adult world. They are unable to communicate with their parents in a meaningful way. With heavy numbers of students to service, teachers and counselors are overworked and often inaccessible. So often a child with a problem goes without help, and a small problem may become a large one. These youngsters could benefit from a tutor or mentor to work with them on a one-to-one basis, provided this individual is carefully selected and oriented.

 • **There are youngsters who, even as early as the first grade and definitely by the time they are teens, seem to be irretrievable.** Some of them are unresponsive to any gesture of help or goodwill. They often reject mentors and shrug off any offer to help them improve in their studies.

In fact, I probably alienated a sizable percentage of those youngsters sitting behind me on their sixth-grade graduation day when, in announcing the Risers program, I said, "It isn't going to be easy. The responsibility for success will lie with you more than with anyone else. Nobody can do this for you. Nobody can study for you, learn for you, or go to school for you, do homework for you, or pass tests for you. These are just some of the things you will have to do on your own. No one can take these responsibilities for you."

I realize now that these words probably turned off at least one-fifth of the class, and they never got turned on again. They were probably thinking, "Six years—geez, what a long time to wait—and all that hard work! I'm tired of school now. What's college about, anyhow?" Only four out of the entire group have ever had a relative in college.

It was the challenge of the Riser program to influence such unmotivated youngsters to go on to a higher level of thinking. This was not easy with kids whose parents had never finished high school, and in whose families there had never been anyone to attend, much less graduate from, college. We did reach most of them, put them on the right track, and kept them there. Those few others—I can only pray for them.

• **Schools must do more to encourage parental education and involvement.** Nothing is more important in the education and development of a child than good parents. The two dozen of our highest achievers among the Risers had involved parents and a positive home environment, no matter their economic level. Some were single mothers, strong and determined, who fully realized the value "Tell Them We Are Rising" offered. Many were employed and contributed, in an independent way, to the progress of their families. Other successful pupils were fortunate enough to have "intact" homes, with a father and mother present to provide the support and guidance that emotionally and socially fragile adolescents need.

Many of our children were born to teenage mothers who lacked the maturity and the knowledge to successfully rear those children. Products of the welfare syndrome, they often repeated the process. There are programs, fortunately, that give special attention to teenage mothers. More programs are needed, for both the teen mother and the teen father.

   • **There can be no letup in reform and restructuring efforts in public education.** In recent years, the most hopeful development has been efforts to make these huge inner-city comprehensive high schools, often referred to as warehouses, more "user friendly." The goal is to break these schools into smaller units, known as charters, where children and teachers begin to develop a comfortable familiarity with each other and their academic subjects. Worthwhile approaches being tried in the charters include longer class periods, interdisciplinary classes, and repetition of material during classes to make sure everyone "gets it"—not too far from the approach I used as a neophyte teacher. Hopefully, this will lead to higher rates of academic success and lower dropout rates.

   Results so far are tentative but encouraging. Many of our Risers, with serious problems both academic and personal, were getting higher grades in their subjects and passing more courses in these reconfigured schools. Staff development and joint lesson planning are features that the teachers in charter schools approve, since they feel their knowledge of their kids is finally being taken into account.

   It will be fascinating to see if such initiatives become standard issue among the nation's schools, particularly in the cities where staggering amounts of money have been pledged to the effort to create them. Billionaire publisher and philanthropist Walter H. Annenberg has bestowed a $50-million challenge grant in New York and similar sums in Philadelphia, Chicago, and Los Angeles, some of which will help open small charter schools or help convert the large schools into charters.

• **We must learn not to write off anyone.** People are unpredictable. Just when you think you have someone all figured out, the person changes. And this has been true of the Risers. Several who dropped out, got pregnant, or were incarcerated in juvenile facilities came back into the fold, albeit a year or two behind the others, determined to at least finish high school, possibly to take advantage of "Grandma's" college tuition offer.

I think of the kids labeled "special" who are often not retarded at all—just treated that way by a system too clogged to individualize instruction. If we can find the right instructional programs for them, I believe there is no limit to their achievement. Some effort has been made in this direction with the I.E.P. (Individualized Education Program), but I do not know how effective it has been.

We must realize that it takes all kinds to make up this world. There are many talents beyond the purely academic ones of reading, writing, and mathematics. Think about those folks who probably could not score above the fiftieth percentile—that magical Maginot Line—on the national standardized tests in the so-called basic skills, but are blessed with mechanical expertise or a creative talent in art, music, interior decoration, dress design, crafts, or carpentry. And those with immeasurable talents in human relationships—compassion, leadership, patience, the capacity to love and commitment to serve.

As principal at William Penn High School for Girls in the '50s and early '60s, in recurring assemblies I would remind the student body, "Each and every one of you is a beautiful person, and moreover, each and every one of you has some very special talent. The trick is discovering that talent and developing it." Yes, this kind of talk did help many a student improve her self-image.

I think of Brody (not his real name), one of the nation's most outstanding artists. As a Philadelphia elementary school student he was labeled OB, or orthogenic backward, as the retarded were classified in those days. He demonstrated a gift for drawing and painting at an early age. Yet he was put into a "special-ed" class in spite of the fact that he had a clearly demonstrated talent—his pictures were hanging all over the school. The principal, God rest his sorry soul, insisted that Brody was genuinely retarded.

"Oh yes, he can draw and paint. Sort of an aberration. But the boy is a retard. No college will ever admit him."

Well, the highly respected and nationally renowned Academy of Fine Arts did indeed admit this gifted young man, and in his second year he won the highly coveted Cresson Fellowship for a year of travel abroad.

His professor at the academy later told me the principal seemed determined to spread the claim of retardation when references for admission to the academy were solicited. But it was a real smear. Not only was Brody a gifted artist, he displayed an analytical, critical mind and had no problem coping with the academic side of college work.

How often are our children mislabeled "special-education" students to languish in classrooms and with teachers who make little effort to probe their potential strengths and talents! Of the twenty-six of my own Risers labeled in sixth grade as "special-ed" pupils, ten were placed in regular classes in ninth grade. Six subsequently graduated from high school with a standard diploma. Two are enrolled in college.

• **Programs like "Tell Them We Are Rising" make a difference.** Without my leap of faith, without the intervention of the Risers program, I believe the overwhelming majority of these children would have been swept away into the underbelly of society via drugs, illiteracy, unwed motherhood, and the other social ills that plague their peers. A Temple University study of Risers measured them against their true peers, those who graduated from the same elementary schools a year earlier. Of the latter, 48.7 percent, almost half, dropped out of school, while only 33 percent of those who began in the Risers dropped out. Only 3.5 percent of the non-Risers have no grades below B—in other words, honor-roll caliber—compared with 5.2 percent of the Risers.

Dr. Trevor Sewell, dean of Temple University's School of Education, believes that the Risers ultimately will prove "that a similar investment in such kids, kids without the middle-class work habits that most American children have, would cut truancy and dropout rates. Many of the so-called at-risk kids are capable of a better academic performance, but they are not getting the motivation and the positive peer pressure that the Risers get. The Risers are learning the close relationship between educational achievement and high vocational goals, and that connection will make them successful." And with that assessment, I heartily concur.

• **There is a deep sense of personal fulfillment in "giving back."** To have been a part, even though limited, of the lives of 116 young human beings during these past years has been incredibly stimulating and inspiring and probably—I'll say it again—helped prolong my life.

I fervently hope that my Risers have learned, from my example and the example of the caring adults in their lives, the "giving back" to each other. Our common racial

In 1992, the "Tell Them We Are Rising" program was recognized by the
Philadelphia City Council.

identity alone did not, and does not, assure that the once
standard practice of "giving back" that informed African
American lives will be automatically passed on. I hope
they will see the program as a gift of many givers and remember fondly the mentors, their program coordinator
Mrs. Deloris James, the volunteer unpaid speakers and
guides, the tutors and the others—and those principals
and teachers who were most supportive.

For by whatever name it is known, and in whatever
century it is practiced, black people here have helped each
other first, last, and always. The Risers benefited from
some of the finest practitioners—unsung heroes and hero-
ines—of the skill, and the art, of "giving back."

A Final Word

A M I SAD, and sometimes even guilt-ridden, that I could not help more of the original band of 116? Yes.

Am I still puzzled by the ones who I thought were on the right track and ready to make gains but who chose to turn away from that road? Yes.

Do I wish I had turned my hand to some cause other than that of educating children, our most vulnerable citizens, and particularly the neediest, least respected children among us? Absolutely not.

I have gained much more than I sought to give, and learned much more than I could have taught in these fifty-plus years.

As for my life as a whole, outside the professional satisfactions, I am content. I have been blessed with an abundance of love, most recently from my Risers, and I do not doubt that such a blessing is the most anyone can receive on this earthly plane.

Truly I am among the fortunate ones who can say that with all its ups and downs, my life has been a gift, although one wrapped with ribbons of hard work and pain.

These years with my adopted adolescents have proved a worthy coda to a lifelong educational adventure. This period has, as you have seen, taught me more in some ways—and confirmed much of what I have known for decades—about modern America than fifty years in the public schools did, and certainly has taught me more about what it means to this nation if we the people continue to turn our backs on children such as these.

My time with these ambassadors to the future has proven heartbreaking, stimulating, and exhilarating at the same time. I thought I was so aware and so sophisticated about the dangers, the pitfalls, facing these children, but I learned so much more.

The lives of the Risers, from their rocky origins to their fledgling-adult status, not only contradict the conventional picture of these children as hopeless cases, but also contradict my own life experience as an adolescent, and some of my professional experience as a teacher of adolescents in 1950s America. This experience has made me reevaluate what I thought about life and how best to prepare a child for life as a productive citizen and hopefully a happy one.

And I have been made humble by the sight of so much pure, unadulterated hope for a better life—accompanied, at times, by unrealistic expectations, to be sure—that predominates among my Risers, these same children whom politicians cluck over as hopeless and others scorn as worthless. Individually and collectively, they have stirred so much in me. I have been touched by all of them.

Index